00087866

179.409 VIV

D0610593

/

This book is due for

A CAT IN HELL'S CHANCE

The story of the campaign against
Hill Grove cat farm

written by
the campaigners

edited by
Anny Malle

SLINGSHOT PUBLICATIONS
London
2002

A Cat in Hell's Chance
The story of the campaign against Hill Grove cat farm.
First published November 2002.
© Slingshot Publications 2002
BM Box 8314 London WC1N 3XX

Type set by Viviana D. Guinarte
In Times New Roman 11/12, Book Antiqua 10/11, Century
Schoolbook, Helvetica, Sand, Andale Mono, and B Times Bold.
Printed in Spain.
Cover designed by Andy Dark.
Cover photographs: The Oxford Mail, Andy Dark, and
Hidden Crimes photographic exhibition
www.novisezione.org/mostra/index_en.html

British Library Cataloguing in Publication Data
Written by The Campaigners, edited by Anny Malle
A Cat in Hell's Chance: The story of the campaign against
Hill Grove cat farm.
1. Hill Grove Farm. 2. Cats as laboratory animals – England.
3. Animal experimentation – England. 4. Anti-Vivisection – England.
1. Title 179.4'0942

ISBN   0-9519646-2-3

This book is sold subject to the condition that it shall not,
as a whole, or in parts, by way of trade or otherwise,
be lent, resold, hired out, or otherwise circulated without
the publisher's prior consent in any form of binding
or cover other than that in which it is published
and without a similar condition
being imposed upon the subsequent purchaser.
Selected non continuous pieces may be quoted
in reviews and other works, leaflets or pamphlets.

Half the profits from the sale of this book
will go to the cause of abolition of vivisection
on scientific and medical grounds.

Dedication

This book is dedicated to all those both at home and abroad who give their time and energy to the liberation of animals. The book acknowledges and honours all those who have been arrested or spent time in police cells or prison specially during the campaign to save the cats at Hill Grove: Sue Amos, Mel Arnold, Greg Avery, Lisa Benzing, Bob Byot, Stephen Caine, Bill Dale, Peter Merson-Davies, Jamail Eboe, Adam Gould, Rebecca Green, Stephen Greenwood, Kievan Hickey, Paul Holliday, David Lakeman, Rodrigo López, Annie Malle, Adam Marshall, Stephen Massey, Greg Matthews, Anna Monaghan, Thomas Monaghan, Wendy Nikolaou, Sylvia O'Bricn, Guy Rees, Lucy Richards, Karen Rodgers, Timothy Senior, Ben Thompson, Annette Tibbles, Andrew Wassley, and Anne Marie Moynihan who served two prison sentences.

The book is also dedicated to 31 year old Jill Phipps who on February 1st 1995 paid the ultimate price campaigning for veal calves about to be transported abroad from Coventry. Jill's Mother, Nancy, was a protestor at Hill Grove and all the Phipps family continue to work for animal liberation.

Acknowledgements

The editor wishes to thank the following for their valuable assistance: Cynthia O'Neill who gave her time for interviews; Roger Lee who spent many hours translating and typing pieces of handwriting; Jill who proof read the work; Viviana who typeset the manuscript and Martin Walker who prepared the book for publication. I would also like to thank three of my lecturers, Bob, Ted and Carol, who gave their time to discuss how all the disjointed personal accounts might be turned into a book. The book would never have got off the ground without a generous gift from the estate of the late Ron Shirvell and a small legacy from another animal lover. We thank the following newspapers for their kindness in allowing publication of news items and photographs: Daily Mail, Sunday Express, Oxford Courier Newspapers, Oxford County Newspapers, Sunday People, Cotswold Standard.

Finally, we have to thank the protesters who took the trouble to send in their stories, photographs and often-anonymous gifts to contribute to the publication. And all the others whose work and commitment closed Hill Grove, especially those who are not mentioned by name in the book.

CONTENTS

Part Three
The Struggle Intensifies
105

Foreword

In 1883 Victor Hugo exclaimed: "Vivisection is a crime!" Since then this crime has collected all the superlatives; it is the most horrible crime, the longest ongoing, the biggest numerically and to many the most disturbing. It is as well the greatest money spinner, the best kept secret, and perhaps the most notorious legal crime, blessed by both the Church and the State. Vivisection is a morally accepted practice, so says the Catechism of the Catholic Church.[1]

Vivisection is the crime most in need of abolition and I mean total abolition, because no good can come from such evil. Don't accept the vivisectors attempts to put to sleep public opinion by talking about lessening the numbers or mitigating the pain. There can be no reforming vivisection. No sane person would talk about reforming methods of torture or re-designing concentration camps; would they? It is the moral duty of every human being who deserves this qualification, to fight vivisection with every heartbeat.

Don't ever believe that you cannot do something about it. 2000 years ago Christ said to his Apostles: "If you have faith, you can tell this mulberry tree, 'lift yourself up with your roots and plant yourself in the sea' and it will do it!". Cynthia O'Neill is a person who has proved that apparently impossible things can become reality. She stood up against intimidation, physical vio-

---

1 Paragraph 2417.

lence, death threats, poisoning and the destruction of her belongings in her fight to close the cat breeding centre at Hill Grove farm; nothing diverted Cynthia from her goal.

Without Cynthia, cat farmer Christopher Brown would still be selling kittens to the torture labs. "Bred to purrfection for over 25 years", as he advertised in the *Laboratory Animals Buyers Guide* in 1996. Those involved in vivisection stick together forming a kind of secret society which encompasses: the breeders, the pharmaceutical companies, vivisection laboratories, the producers of cages and special test equipment, ground transporters as well as many international airlines which still fly almost any species of primate and other animals into the hell of vivisection laboratories in Europe, the United States, and the rest of the world.[2]

Together with the apparently more reputable vivisection support organisations, there are the especially despicable animal stealing organisations. Each year alone in France, more than 65,000 dogs and cats are stolen and sold to the vivisection sadists. As the famous German psychotherapist Dr. Herbert Stiller put it: "Vivisectors are a special kind of being, one should not carelessly call them human!". Cynthia O'Neill knew what she was up against when she decided to make a stand against the horror.

In this book you can see the setbacks Cynthia suffered. The intrigues of which she became a victim, the injustices, the hardship, the deceptions, the wall of administrative rules and regulations, followed to the letter by the police. You can see as well, the way she progressed in her struggle for justice, through the steady increase in the number of supporters to the joy of the final victory. As spokesman for numerous anti-vivisection associations, I would like to thank Cynthia O'Neill and all the

---

2 A campaign has been waged for years now by activists in Israel and supporters in other countries against the breeding and the transport of primates from Israel to other countries. The campaign has taken legal action against a number of airlines to try to stop transportation.

wonderful people in Great Britain, as well as animal protectors all over the Continent and overseas, as far away as New Zealand, who gave valuable support to this courageous, determined and outstanding defence of God's voiceless creations!

Hans Fischinger [3]*, Sainte Maxime, Southern France. May, 2000*

---

3 Hans Fischinger died at his home on December 25 2001 after a life committed to animal liberation. He was instrumental in getting many German, French and Swiss activists to help in the early days of the Hill Grove campaign.

Preface

In 1991, following the disappearance of her cat Snowy, in broad daylight from the garden of her Oxfordshire home, Cynthia O'Neill became determined to act against vivisection. She soon found that her cat was not the only one in the area to disappear. She now thinks that every year, hundreds of cats are stolen and sold to laboratories, in Oxfordshire alone.

Despite the fact that the cat wore a name and address tag, offers of a large reward, the circulation of handbills and posters, local radio reports and requests from listeners, no one found Cynthia's cat or the one belonging to her neighbour, which disappeared on the same day. It was from Cynthia O'Neill's involvement with the people that she met while searching for her cat that a small group of people got together and began to research the use of cats for experimentation in Oxford.[4] This group then embarked upon a campaign against the use of cats in experiments.[5]

---

4 I was told that some younger activists got into one of the cancer research labs in Oxford. The freezers contained mutilated animals, amongst them a pure white cat, identical and of the same age as Cynthia's cat Snowy.

5 Cynthia O'Neill's campaign against vivisectors at Oxford University began when she read about the work of Professor Blakemore at the Departments of Psychology and Physiology at Oxford University, which involved the sewing up of cats' eyes. On her visit to the labs searching for her cat, Cynthia says that, though she was not abusive or threatening in any way, she and her companion were met with a police car and soon afterwards a police helicopter appeared overhead! "Get out, it's none of your business", the doorman shouted at her.

Cynthia first reported her suspicions about the theft of her cat to the police, who failed to act. "It was strange", she said, "how they can justify spending millions to stop cats being rescued from labs, breeding farms etc. but are unable even to make eye contact with someone who reports the theft of an animal".[6]

From Oxford, the group's campaign focused on gathering information about Hill Grove farm. With the excuse of looking for her cat Cynthia visited the farm in November 1991. On this visit, Cynthia found herself face to face with Mr Brown, Katherine, his wife, and their son:

> *I was lectured by the Browns on the great value of their cats in the production of cat vaccines and how their cats were finding cures for human illnesses. Their words were confident but at the same time I felt that they were on the defensive!*

> *I must say I left the farm feeling that perhaps I was misguided. Looking back, I think that perhaps the Research Defence Society or some similar organisation had briefed them on what to say and how to deal with inquisitive visitors.*

Cynthia O'Neill is the first to admit that, at this time in 1991, she was very much a 'raw beginner.' She had not even heard of *Slaughter of the Innocent* by Hans Ruesch, the book that has informed the anti-vivisection movement for many years. In fact, the beginnings of Cynthia's involvement in the Hill Grove campaign, she was to realise, later bore an odd resemblance to Hans Ruesch's own induction searching for his stolen dog.

Like some other campaigning books written on a shoe string, this one has a chequered history. When the campaign to close Hill Grove was over, most of the participants returned to their normal

---

6 Cynthia drew my attention to the Park Farm stolen dogs saga, in which the police had preferred to turn a blind eye. Owned by Oxford University, Park Farm , was raided by the ALF in 1985 and stolen pet dogs were discovered.
Park Farm was raided by the ALF in 1985 and stolen pet dogs were discovered. One activist described the farm as "A filthy place!".

lives and few of them had the desire to write about the experience. I had been intermittently involved in the Hill Grove campaign throughout the years of my PhD studies in Oxford; I knew Cynthia O'Neill and some of the other campaign-ers. Some notes and individual pieces of writing had already been gathered and a basic narrative written, mainly due to Cynthia's energy. When this energy and that of others finally ran out, I was approached and asked to write up the campaign.

The book is both an account of the campaign to shut down Hill Grove cat farm and a tribute to Cynthia O'Neill, who through the campaign became committed to the cause of anti-vivisection. In order to write the book I recorded many hours of conversation with Cynthia and other campaigners.

Once the heat of battle has cooled, it is relatively hard to assemble an objective account of a campaign. I have tried my best to work with the different material given to me and gathered later by me in interviews. I have tried to be as consistent as possible but I have been unable to avoid using a variety of different styles. Not wanting to write a formal history, I have collaged these contributions together in what I think is the most appropriate way.

Anny Malle, Oxford 2002

PETA estimated from the EPA's own figures that these tests will use "between 600,000 and 1.2 million animals to test all 1,000 chemicals". PETA says that this enormous programme is moving ahead "despite widespread criticism from the scientific, regulatory, and even some within the environmental community". In the European countries, new toxicity trials for known toxic chemicals are scheduled to maim, torture and kill 50 million animals.[8,9]

I hope if someone wanted to get to know me he would not bash me on the head, cut my brain out of my head, take my head from my neck, cut my body in half, turn me upside down, burn me with acid, and torture the whole and all the bits with electricity and God knows what... I don't see how we can expect to get away with tormenting our fellow creatures in the ways we do without the evil method (practice) corrupting our ways of construing what we are doing (theory)".[10]

In the eighteenth century all scientists agreed that human vivisection was a completely unacceptable "violation of the laws, not only of divinity but humanity".[11]

In the late 1940s and again in the early 1950s, Massachusetts Institute of Technology scientists conducting research fed breakfast food containing... radioactive iron and calcium... to "mentally retarded" children. The National Institutes of Health, the Atomic Energy Commission, and the Quaker Oats company funded the research.[12]

Defenders of industrial progress are either blind or corrupt if they pretend that they can calculate the price of progress. The torts resulting from Nemises cannot be compensated, calculated or liquidated.[13]

Socialism says: "Work, laugh, love, and don't forget the sparrows." [14]

8 Voluntary Children's Chemical Evaluation Program, set up by the US Environmental Agency, to give the chemical companies the "opportunity" to "voluntarily" test toxic chemicals.

9 The Civil Abolitionist, vol. 13, issue 2. (See contact in Appendix 2).

10 R. D. Laing 1976, *The Facts of Life*, Harmondsworth, England.

11 R. Boyle (1744) cited in *Vivisection in Historical Perspective*, Ed. Nicolas A. Rupke. Routledge, London 1987.

12 *Final Report of the Advisory Committee on Human Radiation Experiments*. Oxford University Press. New York , 1996.

13 Ivan Illich, *Medical Nemesis: The expropriation of health*. Calder and Boyer, 1975.

14 A. Neil Lyons, in Robert Blatchford. *The Sketch of a Personality: An Estimate of Some Achievements*. The Clarion Press. London, 1910.

Prologue

A Reputable Business?

I was once told by a research scientist in Oxford that she "got through" several cats a day in the course of her work. They were all conscious and squealing. She told me that she had been working in the labs for 15 years and had never made a discovery, which could be described as useful to the human race. It was, she said blithely, just "pure science".[1]

Until animal liberation activists came along, no one had suggested that the Hill Grove cat-breeding farm was anything other than a reputable business and Christopher Brown anything more than a small businessman, getting by, making a living. In fact before Christopher Brown started breeding cats he had been a progressive farmer. His wife Katherine's father was a veterinary surgeon and in the early nineteen seventies he had lent his support to Katherine and Christopher's idea of setting up a model farm.

Christopher Brown says that he and his wife wanted kids to come and stay on the farm and learn about animals. They did not, he says, like the idea of city kids believing that milk grew in bottles and thought they could come to Hill Grove farm and mix with and observe animals. The Browns were sure that they could develop the smallholding, which they had acquired in Minster Lovell near the village of Witney in Oxfordshire. They planned to use one of the cottages adjacent to the farmhouse as a dormitory.

---

1 A. N. Wilson, quoted in *Oxford Times*, August 20, 1999.

When, however, Mr Brown presented the idea to the local council for planning permission it was refused on the grounds that it would generate too much traffic along Dry Lane, the small road that ran past the farm. In the face of this set back, the Browns thought that a farm bed and breakfast might fulfil a similar function, bringing families with children to the country to stay on a "real farm".

The bed and breakfast business did not generate an enormous amount of money and it was around this time that someone put Christopher Brown in touch with the Medical Research Council.[2] The Medical Research Council wanted live animals bred for testing and experimentation. Brown later agreed, that he had taken up the option of breeding cats in virus-free conditions for research purposes, as a means of boosting farm income.

At that time, research was under way to develop a vaccine to combat the feline equivalent of enteritis. Brown's interest in vaccines was real; some years later he was to tell journalists, "my father suffered from polio. I have seen him with it all my life. Of course people are now vaccinated and there is no fear of it."

Katherine and Christopher Brown decided that they would breed cats for medical research. They got planning permission for the building of sheds on the farm and they began breeding in sterile conditions in the mid-seventies. Once they had begun they found a ready market for their cats. Of course it was not possible to know exactly what happened to all their cats, but they understood that in the main they were used for useful research into human and animal medicine; one reassuring factor was that they knew much work had to be done on cat viruses and their cats were obviously ideal for this.

---

2 At that time a solely government funded research establishment which dispersed funding to in house and outside research scientists doing research on a wide variety of public health issues.

By the 1980s the Brown's business was doing well and they were breeding hundreds of kittens, which they distributed to laboratories across England and abroad.

Breeding animals for vivisection is, however, different in the public mind from breeding animals for food. A large number of people find vivisection revolting and many also believe that it is unscientific and ultimately detrimental to human health. While Mr Brown and his family viewed their cat breeding as a reputable business, others believed that to breed cats and use them to test cosmetics and household products or torture them for the sake of "pure science" was wholly disreputable.

In the mid-nineties information came to light about how cats bred in sterile conditions like those at Hill Grove farm were used. Breeding records showed that a male 90g kitten was sent to an English university on January 10th 1994 when he was five weeks old. *The Journal of Neuroscience* showed for the same period that a professor from that university used kittens between two and 143 days old in brain experiments. They were blinded in one eye, anaesthetised and put in a head frame while their brain was injected with a dye. They were then destroyed and their brains dissected.

Also during this time, the methods of breeding cats came under criticism; "breeding queens" were put in cages with tomcats and when they became pregnant housed in a birthing shed. They would have their kittens taken from them and sold a few weeks after birth (in some cases at just 13 days old). The breeding queen would then be returned to the toms. The ten-year life of a breeding queen would be spent continuously in this way, like a birthing factory, and then she would be killed.

Because cats for experiment are raised in sterile conditions, they have to be born by Caesarean operations. Cats brought up in breeding sheds suffer many of the same problems as chickens brought up in battery cages or other animals, intensively reared or permanently confined in small spaces. The cats born on Hill Grove farm had a high level of death after birth. One in 10 cats died or were killed by their mothers before they could be reared and sold. Many kittens were born deformed and were destroyed, others were listed in farm records as "eaten", maimed or killed by the mother.

As a licensed breeder, Mr Brown had a close relationship with the Home Office which granted his licence and which also, in troubled times, helped him and other breeders for vivisection with ideological, business help and support. Although New Labour pledged to end vivisection before they came to office, in power they backtracked on this commitment. The closeness of New Labour to international pharmaceutical and biogenetic companies has meant their continuing commitment to animal breeding for experimentation and vivisection.

Cats shock down on holiday farm

Animal lovers are fighting to get a farm struck off the tourist board's approved list for family holidays. For farmer Christopher Brown, apart from offering bed and breakfast holidays, also breeds cats for laboratory experiments. Hundreds of anti-vivisectionists have now signed a petition calling for the tourist board to act.

Mr Brown's 80 acre Hill Grove farm at Minster Lovell, Nr Burford, Oxfordshire, is advertised in a Thames and Chilterns Tourist Board leaflet. The leaflet says the farm rears beef cattle, chickens and ducks and "welcomes children of all ages". It does not mention that the farm has facilities to breed at least 400 cats a year in almost germ free conditions. Each cat is sold for £75 to £110, providing the £6 a night holiday farm with a potential extra income of around £36,000 a year.

As a registered and accredited lab breeder, Mr Brown has to raise his cats in sterile conditions with special ventilation to keep them virtually germ free. All have to be born by Caesarean operations. So far, the Tourist Board have refused to act on the animal lovers' protests.

A spokesman for the Thames and Chilterns Tourist Board said: "As long as this doesn't interfere with the bed and breakfast service, it is none of our business." When the Sunday People visited Mr Brown's farm last week, he was off on his own holiday for two weeks. But he has been quoted in the local press as saying: "I don't do anything which I would consider to be cruel to animals. We breed cats for research into vaccines, which will save animals' lives".

Sunday People, **August 9ᵗʰ 1981**

I do not wish to answer that question

Apart from the fact that Animal Liberation activists were gathering on the perimeter of the farm, in all other respects it was an ordinary September night. The rain had caused the footpath over the fields to be muddy and slippery.

Most of the activists who drove through the night to Hill Grove farm, on Wednesday the 23rd September 1981, had had a good meal and a bath before they set out; sooner or later they would be caught and they wanted to be prepared. The activists knew the risks involved; they knew as well that the police already had their eye on several of them.

That year, television and newspapers had been reporting the growth of ALF[3] in many successful raids. They exposed Laundry Farm in Cambridge, discovering stolen pet dogs. Nippy, a dog from Rotherham, was traced by the ALF to a Leeds University lab and in a daring raid on Sheffield University in 1980, activists rescued a black Labrador and returned him to his grateful owners.

If the Brown family had seen the article "Cats shock down on the Farm" in the *Sunday People*[4] they probably still felt secure; nothing could happen in the sleepy village of Minster Lovell, could it?

---

3 The Animal Liberation Front, made up of men and women of all ages, from all walks of life, all of whom are willing to go to prison for their beliefs. These activists chose to do a little bit more, sometimes attempting to liberate animals from labs and breeding establishments.

4 *Sunday People* August 9, 1981.

Peter and Maggie arrived at the farm that night in a green Mini van emblazoned with a 'Special Deliveries' sign, driven by Paddy attired in a National Carrier's uniform. A note in the front of the van stated that it was legally carrying 27 lots of animals to an address in Hampshire. In the back were cat baskets, torches, gloves, wire cutters and nylon bags to carry cats. Telephone numbers were safely written where they could not be seen, on the activist's arms. Peter and Maggie waited patiently until everyone was in place.

In the quiet, eerie darkness nine activists quickly crossed the path at the back of the farm, cut the wire fence and with one wrench of a jemmy, swung open the heavy door of the first breeding shed. Making a noise was risky but it was the only way to get in.

Once inside the cat shed, the activists saw cats and kittens crammed together like battery chickens. One activist counted over 70 cats in an 8 by 5 foot cage. They lost no time in looking through the paper work and were shattered to learn of the fate of the cats. This most valuable ALF raid was to prove beyond doubt that these cats were not used for testing cat foods, nor were they sent for cat vaccine research. The majority ended up in atrocious experiments. Why were Shell Petroleum, Porton Down, Smith-Kline Beecham, I.C.I., Glaxo and other companies buying cats from the farm? The hastily collected papers also revealed, in small part, what kind of experiments were performed on the cats. In one described experiment a mother cat's limbs were amputated to learn how she would continue to look after her kittens.

Speed was of the essence; working as quickly as possible, gloved hands picked up crying cats. In the rushed chaotic darkness, at two in the morning, one of the liberators activated the alarm. Brown was anyway out of bed by this time, after hearing a noise; he had got dressed and was making his way over to the breeding buildings accompanied by two dogs. Checking the units he found the door to number 3 unit open: he quickly locked and bolted it, bringing up a tractor to keep it shut, trapping the activists inside.

Witney Police were quick to respond to the alarm, they came rushing onto the farm with a police dog. At two fifty, the activists were all led out of the breeding unit. They had, they estimated, left behind nine hundred cats. With the provision of minimal facilities for the cats and only minimal human contact, these prize "laboratory tools" looked like a good "crop" for the farmer.

As she was led into the police van, Maggie thought only that she had let down the cats, the eyes and cries of the ones she had reached down and put into a bag, filling her heart with grief.

Eleven activists, 'The Curbridge Eleven', were charged with trespassing in a cat-breeding unit with intent to steal, contrary to the 1968 Theft Act. Just in case the police found it hard to prove the substantive charge –nothing had actually been stolen– charges of "conspiracy to steal" were also brought against the eleven.

At the farm itself, Det. Constable Paul Faulkner, who affected the arrests with the help of his police dog said, "I am arresting all nine of you on suspicion of burglary." Maggie replied "You're supposed to be a fair-minded man. Go in there and have a look at the conditions he keeps those cats in. You'll realise that he is the villain and not us. It's disgusting the way those cats are kept."

The activists acquitted themselves well in the police station, each one answering all the questions addressed to them with the words "I do not wish to answer that question". On May 21, 1982 the defendants were brought before Oxford County Court; dressed in their smartest clothes they attempted to show the court how ordinary and decent they were.

The campaigners told the jury they wanted to rescue the animals as an act of compassion after they saw a report of the farm's activities in a Sunday newspaper. They said it was a publicity stunt to get the unit closed down and they planned later to leave the cats in the care of the authorities.

Following a four-day trial, attended by animal liberation activists from all over Britain, the jury found the nine defendants guilty and the Judge handed out fines ranging from £50 to £200. Maggie and Peter, both Vauxhall Car workers, received £400 fines; with no legal aid, their legal fees came to over £1500. Despite the financial cost and the fact that they collected criminal records, the couple still believed they were right to try to rescue the cats.

Cynthia's morning 1997

It was bitterly cold with a piercing wind. So cold that, as they spoke, their misty breath filled the air between them like steam. It was a Tuesday morning in February 1997 and the sun had not yet risen.

Cynthia O'Neill had been waiting in her old car with the heater turned on full blast. She was parked on the grass verge in Dry Lane next to Hill Grove farm's private driveway. At twenty minutes past six, out of the pitch darkness exactly as promised, a pair of car headlights flashed and she knew that Natasha was ready for work.

"Watcha! Isn't it cold," said Natasha shivering.

"You bet, I'm freezing," Cynthia replied, pulling her scarf over her face and drawing her jacket hood even tighter. Clutching the megaphone and leaning on her walking frame Cynthia got down to business.

Only a few hours before, Natasha had achieved the difficult rescue of a mother cat and kittens for the Cats Protection League; someone had dumped the animals near a busy railway line.

On this morning, their task job was to observe the staff arriving at the cat-breeding establishment and note any suspicious vans entering. As in so many other places, cat theft was rife in the area.

The megaphone, which they shared, had a quarter of a mile range and had been obtained by public subscription in memory of deceased pets – the names of Peter a budgy, Bacchus a dog, Fred a cat were just some of those with which it was inscribed. That morning it was put to good use. As each worker arrived they were greeted with "Stop working at Hill Grove farm. Experiments on cats are useless to the human patient."

Natasha quoted the words of Professor Feldberg, the well-known London vivisector,[5] "Being a vivisector is like being a criminal." Dawn broke slowly, but by then both women were fully awake. "Vivisection is a Scientific and Medical Fraud", Cynthia yelled as loudly as possible in the hope that the guests in the Bed and Breakfast on the farm could hear! They made a good attempt at educating and shaming the staff of about twelve, who quite clearly did not appreciate this small but effective demonstration. Cynthia had been conducting this picket as part of a general campaign for almost five years.

"Bye Natasha, thanks a hundred! See you at the car boot sale on Saturday", said Cynthia's, already thinking ahead to the weekend's money raising.

What a relief it was to be back in the comfort of a warm car.

5 During an undercover videotaped investigation which finally exposed the vivisector at the age of 89, Feldberg stated: "How fortunate are those who can do research their whole life, for however long they live, they die young. It keeps you alive. Same as if you were a criminal and enjoy your crimes, it keeps you alive." [*Caught in the Act; The Feldberg Investigation,* by Melody McDonald].

Part One

Cynthia's War

13

Chapter One

🐈 Proper Channels I

In 1834 the local Magistrates in the village of Tolpuddle in Dorsetshire issued placards warning the labourers that anyone joining the union would be sentenced to seven years transportation.[1]

Many serious and far-reaching campaigns have been begun by one person. Often that person, acting like a kind of starter motor, goes through all the formal channels in an attempt to resolve the problem at hand. When, over the next decade, Cynthia O'Neill was told by judges and others that she should have gone through the proper channels, she smiled to herself.

In 1991 Cynthia was a fifty two year old middle class woman who had been a Queen's nursing sister for most of her life.[2] Once she got the bit between her teeth, Cynthia racked her mind for any approach which might help get Brown's cat farm shut down. She tried every democratic and "proper channel" that was available, all to no avail. She fired off letters and visited decision makers with a fiery gusto. She joined a number of large organisations in order to attend their annual general meetings.

---

1 *Six Heroes in Chains*. Harry Brooks, The Wessex Press 1929. Forword by Rt. Hon. J.H. Thomas M.P.

2 Author of two pictorial publications about health: *A Picture of Health*; *Hospitals and Nursing on Old Picture Post Cards,* Meadow Books 1991, now in its third printing, ISBN 0-9515655-0-8; and *More Pictures of Health: Hospitals and Nursing on Old Picture Post Cards*, Meadow Books 1991, ISBN 0-9515655-1-6.

Cynthia and a small group of other activists founded Witney Animal Rights or WAR. "Yes", Cynthia said, "It would be war all right!" Who else would fight for the animals except ordinary people, animal lovers? Having bearded the Browns in their house, she began with her friend Bill to give out thousands of leaflets from a stall, which they set up in Oxfordshire town centres. Visitors to Oxford, Burford, Witney, Cirencester, Moreton in the Marsh, Stow on the Wold and Cheltenham would frequently see Cynthia, or Bill at the stall.

When early in the campaign Cynthia learned of Professor Blakemore's experiments using cats, Cynthia organised a petition aiming to collect 100,000 signatures. Money from the stall raised the £50 required for printing the petition and more leaflets. Cynthia learned early on that campaigns need funding and the small group of protesters began raising funds at second hand stalls and car boot sales.

One supporter, Ron, sent a small donation regularly from November 1991 until his death in 1999. This constant support was bracing, cards and phone calls before and after lone demonstrations and later court appearances meant a great deal. Often Cynthia would come home after a picket wet, tired and aching to find that the postman had brought another encouraging card or a cheque from Ron. It was good just to know that the support was out there.

On most weekday mornings, with a small group of other campaigners Cynthia turned up outside the Browns' farm. The Browns and their staff, who for years had enjoyed peace, quiet and privacy, were suddenly assailed by voices yelling till they were hoarse. They didn't know then but their peaceful days had ended. Cynthia began tying a banner made from a sheet to a hedge at the farm's entrance. Early in 1992 one worker angry at the sloganeering sheet, produced a sharp knife and, white in the face, tried to slash it to ribbons.

WAR held monthly meetings at a flat in Witney, while out-side CID officers sat in their car ready to follow any new faces. Cynthia was sure, however, that agents were not only outside. Despite her wish to concentrate specifically on Hill Grove farm because "it was right on our own doorstep", at least one of their number, kept objecting and demanding that any campaign was left "until next year". Cynthia wondered at first why he made these frequent objections but soon she understood: the enemy was working hard. When the founding members realised that their group, like so many animal rights groups, had been infiltrated, it was disbanded and its members began organising separately.

With snow sometimes round her feet, wrapped up tightly and with a large handmade placard 'Vivisection is Scientific Fraud', Cynthia picketed Hill Grove farm, dreaming of a land-scape in the shadow of a thousand protesters.

Letters and protestations

As well as the picket, Cynthia and her companions began to send letters and arrange meetings with anyone who they thought might bring change to Hill Grove. In addition to breeding cats, the farm had a caravan site and a Bed & Breakfast business, advertised in many tourist guides as "a friendly place to stay". Cynthia tackled the Advertising Standards Authority. She received many replies from them, all along the same lines:

Thank you for your letter of 9th February 1992. We have considered your complaint and would advise that we see no grounds for ASA intervention in this matter. In our opinion there are no claims in the advertisement that we can object to under the terms of the British Code of Advertising Practice.

In view of the above, if you wish to take the matter further, I would sug-gest that you write direct to the advertisers or seek guidance from your local Trading Standards Department or Citizens Advice Bureau. Their addresses and telephone numbers can be obtained from your Town Hall. Although we cannot assist you further, we thank you for taking the trouble to write to us.

Complaints to the Tourist Board had been made as far back as 1982, when they had avoided dealing with the situation by claiming that the B & B was not connected to the cat farm. Yet, it was clearly a whole business advertised to holidaymakers as 'a mixed farm.' The few cattle, sheep and crops hid the more profitable sale of cats. Several times Cynthia visited the local Thames & Chiltern Tourist Board which did not want to discuss the matter.

Thank you for your letter of 5th April, the contents of which have been noted. You will recall that, when we recently met at our offices, I explained to you our position in respect of the activities that are carried out at Hill Grove farm.

Hill Grove farm is not a member of the Thames & Chilterns Tourist Board. The Board's involvement with the Farm is connected with the owner's participation in the National Inspection Scheme that we administer within our Region on behalf of the English Tourist Board. Our role is to inspect and classify the accommodation offered by the owners and, as such, our Inspector would have no need to know of any additional activities at the farm or inspect other parts thereof.

Under the criteria laid down for the National Accommodation Inspection Scheme, there are no sections for us to assess the work carried out at the farm. The only time we would have cause to take account of this is if we were to receive specific complaints from people using the accommodation about the activities which you have brought to our notice. On checking back through the file it would appear that we have received no complaints about the standard of accommodation offered, nor have there been any about the activities on the farm.

Whilst I can appreciate your concern over the activities carried out on the farm, there is nothing that the Tourist Board can do in this matter. I am sure that, if the activities you describe are being carried out to the extent you claim, they will have been licensed and therefore I would assume that the owners of the farm are complying with the statutory regulations. I am sure there are correct channels that can be followed with the appropriate authorities if you believe there are grounds for a complaint.[3]

As the picket and protests grew and guests came to learn more about the place in which they were holidaying, many left in tears. However, business overall was booming for the Browns, so much so that they had requested planning permission to extend the cat

---

3 Thames & Chilterns Tourist Board. May 6, 1992.

farm. The application was granted at a West Oxfordshire District Council meeting in 1988, having first been agreed in the initial phase by the local Parish Council.

It became known later that the Browns attended the local church with some of the local Parish Councillors. Cynthia described it as a "cosy get-together". Despite this, the Planning Council would say later that in 1988 they honestly had not known what 'cats for vivisection' meant. They soon found out when Cynthia began to attend their meetings.

At the first meeting I sat very ladylike and waited until the question time before raising the vexed question. It came like a bolt from the blue. More was to come! I was fast learning that as in any business there are so many fingers in the pie! My questions raised at the PC meeting were ignored because I was not an actual parishioner.

Having had no success in the meetings, Cynthia began writing letters to the Parish Council.

I should be grateful to receive the courtesy of a reply to my first letter to you. On phoning you I was informed that Councillors had all received a copy of my letter so I of course assumed that any Meeting ran in a business like manner and in fact according to Government guidelines would mention that correspondence had been received and action taken.

It has been proved by many that experiments on animals are useless and fraudulent medical research. Humans actually die due to drugs first being tested on animals. We know that cats from farmer Brown's (your parish) go to labs for most cruel, useless experiments. You all know this now, and that accounted for the rudeness and lack of discussion last Monday. Those that keep silent to wrong doings are as equally responsible as the vivisectors in John Radcliffe Infirmary, other hospitals and the university. I would like a reply to both of my letters and an assurance that the matter will be given proper attention. It is my business.[4]

---

4 Cynthia O'Neill to the Parish Council. August 18, 1992.

A curt post-card was returned by the Parish Council.

When the Council met in August your letter of 8 July 1992 had not been discussed at the meeting as it was still in circulation amongst members due to holidays. However the contents of both your letters were discussed at the September meeting and the Council do not wish to comment.[5]

The local Community Health Council were concerned with the health of the community, so Cynthia determined to ask them why health care in the area necessitated vivisection and the breeding of cats for research. Several times she made the sixty mile round journey in her old car before sitting through what she describes as the "boring chit-chat" of the committee. Often she was the only member of the public present. On the 17th December 1992, Cynthia 'asked' the following 'question' at the Community Health Council.

Madam Chairman, members of the Community Health Council, you may wonder why I make a 60 mile return journey at my own time and expense and I am here yet again. I am disturbed that the Minutes of the September meeting are incorrect and I should like to see a correction. The reason I was compelled to attend the September meeting in person was solely due to the fact that my numerous letters, phone calls to the CHC since March have been ignored.

Having seen a video shown on Channel 4 TV on March 10th 1992 in which a stolen dog was shown in Northmoor, that is the place where sad dogs await their transportation to this hospital for vivisection, and also the fact that my own and close neighbours cats have been stolen. I am very suspicious and have a right to know surely as to where the AHA obtain cats and dogs for research. Tony Stapleton says, "I don't have to tell you where I obtain my items from." Animals are NOT items and deserve some respect.

The continued silence for almost a year makes me ask even more questions especially as I myself saw a large furniture van from Sussex recently unloading many frightened cats to Northmoor. This was NOT a lab van. A police helicopter was chasing me in

5 September 25, 1992.

minutes. These sad animals including cats, dogs, monkeys, rats, mice, pigs, and many others are used in useless, barbaric, filthy and vile experiments, all done behind blackened windows and security doors, and any lab worker that spills the beans may suffer imprisonment.

Many patients in this hospital are in due to errors made from applying drugs first tested on animals. An animal is no model for man, look at Thalidomide.

I ask you all to visit for yourself Park Farm, Northmoor and ask to see the wretched animals, but of course you will not be allowed to. Having seen for myself such conditions it is my moral obligation to inform others. We have photographic evidence that over Bank Holiday staff DO NOT visit to feed the dogs. They are filthy in dirty, cold, unheated concrete kennels. This is the way they treat the poor creatures before vivisection. The labs from what I have read and seen are 100% worse.

This is all a waste of public money when at every CHC meeting we hear of 'No money for this and that.' There is plenty for the vivisector's cruel work and perhaps the Speaker at your last meeting could have told you how much of our money goes on fraudulent research!

Dr. Deswatine, physician, Paris: "Vivisection should be prohibited among all civilised peoples and those that practice it should be severely punished. It is a barbaric practice, cruel, irrational and unnecessary, and from whatever standpoint one looks at it, from the physiological, the practical, the medical or the surgical, as well as the therapeutical and toxicological, one cannot protest strongly enough against those dreadful and disgusting experiments. The vivisector brings dishonour to us and brings shame on science."

Cynthia embarrassed members of the Community Health Council by asking them to state their vested interests. Naturally, the CHC being part of local democracy, none of the members was willing to do so. On other occasions Cynthia took along a big banner to 'show them.'

After attending several meetings of the CHC, Cynthia forced the Chairman to get a working party together to look at the
conditions the dogs were kept in at Northmoor before they even
went for use in Oxford hospital labs. She reflects sceptically now
on such an initiative:

> What to date had been done? You've guessed it. Exactly nil, but
> a letter from CHC asking me to refrain from attending further
> meetings. Albeit these are public meetings paid for by Mr & Mrs
> Joe Bloggs. It has been said that people who get themselves
> elected onto Committees often have vested interests at heart.
> How often this has been proved right!

Increasingly members of the CHC had to listen to the case of
scientific and medical fraud put forward by Cynthia. Ultimately,
they found it easy to fall back on their pride and rather than begin
a serious investigation into Cynthia O'Neill's claims, they tried to
ban her from attending all meetings.

> *Thank you for your postcard. The Chair of CHC, Mrs Mary Judge has*
> *asked me to write to you following the presentation you made at the*
> *end of the last CHC meeting, which was deeply offensive to CHC mem-*
> *bers.*
>
> *In view of this, and in order to prevent any further disruption, a deci-*
> *sion has been taken to ask you not to attend future CHC meetings.*
>
> *Needless to say, the CHC is available to you as to all members of the*
> *public to advise and give information on access to health services for*
> *Oxfordshire residents.*[6]

Fortunately for the Hill Grove cats, the CHC seemed unable to
enforce their edict and had as Cynthia says, "more of Mrs O'Neill
on future agendas."

---

6 Oxfordshire CHC. June 15, 1993.

Chapter Two

🐈 **A Jail Journal**

> *By levying on the time of the prisoner, the prison seems to express in concrete terms the idea that the offence has injured, beyond the victim, society as a whole.*[1]

By the end of 1992 with her gross nuisance value increasing daily, Cynthia found herself getting smacked on the wrist by the authorities. She took this as a sign that she was beginning to be a threat.

In September 1992, Cynthia ended up in police custody for the third time. On this occasion she was wrongly accused of non-attendance at a court hearing. Throughout the three days that she was in custody in Witney and Oxford, she kept a diary, written on various bits of paper with an HMSO black biro. What the diary reveals, more than any cruel oppression, is the way in which the police begin to enact judicial punishments on individuals before Magistrates or Judges have made any sentences. The short diary shows clearly the petty erosion of liberty that can wear unprepared prisoners down and ensure that they return to the security of their ordinary lives.

---

1 Michel Foucault. *Discipline and Punish: The birth of the prison.* Peregrine Books, Harmondsworth England. 1979.

Banbury Police Station 29.8.92

6.00 pm. Arrested, charge not attending court Thursday, re. criminal damage. I ask to get a change of pants. They allow me to get a change of pants and collect books. Am driven to Banbury Station. I ask first if I could phone solicitor as I know a mistake has been made. Get to Banbury. Sgt.very rude. "Please can I see a doctor, I am in your custody and I do not feel well. May I phone my solicitor?" With hands on his hips "We do not want any nuisance from you, I have to complete formalities first. I'm busy and been working all day." I explain again how dazed I feel and how I have to take take Serc[2] at 6.50pm.[3] I feel very cold and shivery. Luckily I have an apple that I can eat with Serc. I tell them I have not had a proper meal all day and feel unwell and not fit to travel. My solicitor phones and the police put me in a filthy, smelly tobacco filled room. I ask for some air. "It is not the Ritz", is the reply. I have to leave the door open as I speak to Solicitor, as smoke is so foul. Gradually feel better and am put in a cell and given a small sheet of writing paper. Solicitor phones again and says that I may be here till Tuesday a.m. They have especially chosen to keep me here over Bank Holiday. Clever, that's the word!

8.10 pm. I ask for my books and paper and to phone my son and the Sgt. says she is dealing with another prisoner, then will get them. Tell them I'm better and can travel. Will be nice to get to Oxford. If I have my books I'll feel better. Lighting here not too good but cell is clean and doesn't smell. Could do with some grub. Am waiting for transport to Oxford. Why do they b***** me around? Clever? Have 2 blankets so feel warmer. Sit on one and cover up with the other. Had a lie down and head feels better. The weather is so very cold for August.

---

2 A therapy for Meniere's disease
3 Cynthia was not well at this time she had a serious heart complaint. She invariably had to use two walking sticks to get around.

8.28 pm. Feel much better now. Still no grub. Windows of cell are blocked by thick glass so of course one has no view. Glad that awful Sgt. is off. Be easier to write leaning on a book. Solicitor said earlier on she can't get to the office until Tuesday. I explain that this is not good enough.

8.40 pm. Still no grub. Am offered coffee, however she says transport will be 20 minutes and then to Oxford and vegetarian food there. Says they can keep us up to 4 hours before feeding. My lovely books arrive. Luxury. I ask for more paper. Perhaps it is cold enough to wear tights. My feet are cold.

8.50 pm. Lady Sgt. brings me a glorious stock of notepaper and cup of coffee. She has a pleasant manner and says she will try and get phone. Will be a long stay if I've got to be in the cells till Tuesday. Can hear ventilation working and cell is not smelly. Feel tired as I've had so busy a day. I had got up early. Picked up Sophie and then to Witney with stall until I got very cold at 1.00 pm. Did some shopping at the supermarket then home. Cook Brendan[4] some cheese and mash and phone goes. Neil itching to placard farmer Brown again so we arrange to meet at Buttercross. Brendan helps with the placards. Very windy and gets cold. Leave Neil at bus stop and get home about 6.00 pm and Old Bill in a car follow me in. Expect my transport will be here any moment. Still no meal and I expect most people will have had an evening meal by 9.00 pm.

9.15 pm. Enjoying reading *A Surgeon's Story* by Stephen K. Westman. Has Sgt. forgotten that I wanted to phone? Had I ever dreamed of arrest today I would certainly have had an evening meal etc. at home.

9.26 pm. Still no transport and no grub. Ring the service bell, Sgt. comes. I say again that due to a busy day I have not had a meal and think 9.30 pm too late. She says I can be in custody 4 hours before being fed regardless of what I've had or not had all day!

---

4 Cynthia's son.

Explains that she has a microwave here and food has to be defrosted etc. I say I've been here quite a while now. Says she can't keep her men hanging around while I eat! The journey to Oxford will be nice and a break. If I was in Witney, Brendan could bring in some fish and chips but I'm away out here for a purpose.

9.34 pm. Oxford will be delayed. "We've put a vegetarian meal in microwave, will be about 15 minutes." Couldn't they have done this earlier? A busy Saturday night one would think police officers valuable time could be more gainfully employed than keeping me behind bars?

9.55 pm. Rattle of keys. "Well Cynthia, the best we can do." "What is it?", "A sort of cauliflower cheese and baked beans. I suggest you try it first." "Thank you, not bad". I eat most of it. Pepper and salt would have been a luxury extra! Doesn't seem to be any afters coming, or coffee. My back and neck are quite sore as no chair to sit on. I lean against the cell wall. Lighting in here not really good enough to read by.

10.25 pm. So glad my inner door not locked but of course the outer one is and I am a PRISONER. How must the dogs, cats and monkeys feel when cooped up in cages and boxes? Would so love a hot bath.

11.30 pm. Arrive at Oxford after a ride in police car by WPC and a male officer. Only have one panadol and take that as my neck is quite sore. Brendan has phoned and they ask me about medicines needed. Police are not allowed to give Panadol. Cell number 14 has very good fluorescent lighting. WPC gives me a blanket and I ask for another. Warmer here but my feet still cold. Home from home. I recognise the graffiti on the walls. I was in this cell on my last visit to Oxford.

11.45 pm. Ring bell… 11.54 pm, ring bell again… 11.58 pm, ring bell… Possibly all bells not working again like Witney. 11.59 pm, ring again. Knock on cell door. Should like my one free call to Brendan and light out, to sleep. Seemed to have a lot of police on duty when I came.

Sunday 30.8.92

12.00 midnight. Ring again. Bang on door. Think the banging of cells is other prisoners requesting help. Using my wooden sandals I again bang door very loudly as I hear police talking. Obvious bell ignored and my calls ignored.

12.07 am. Ring again and bang very loudly with my shoe. "Is there a police officer please"? I call three times. I can hear them talking and it is obvious that they chose not to answer my calls. I could be ill. What do they care? Are they not supposed to check a prisoner every so often?

12.12 am. After calling again WPC comes "I've been extremely busy". "Don't believe that one, I request my one free phone call". "Are you calling me a liar"? "You should answer the bells, people may be ill". Cannot sleep in this strong light anyway.

12.20 am. Ring bell again as I am entitled to one call and Brendan should not be disturbed in the middle of the night and after all I have been arrested now for over 6 hours.

12.25 am. Bell answered by another WPC. Says they have 15 inmates! I say the bell should be seen to sooner than 22 minutes. At last I can speak to Brendan on the phone, it's 1.00 am. I return to my cell. Am given night light. My feet still cold. Will try to get some sleep.

7.30 am. Ring the bell and WPC answers very soon and I ask to speak to a Supt. as I am wrongly arrested and should not be here. I ask for a better light and it is switched on. V.G. A good light is worth a lot.

7.45 am. Duty Sgt. on and says he is the boss and will phone my solicitor and get another blanket for my back. Have a picture of Molly, the beautiful dog used and abused by Glaxo, made to produce puppies and even more puppies for vivisection, and then sold on the cheap to the London Hospital.

7.50 am. Writing this diary is therapeutic. "Here you are." A young officer hands me coffee (very welcome) via the window. I tell him how I shouldn't be here and show him dear Molly. Tears come to my eyes when I think of and look at Molly. She is dead but I know her spirit is in this nasty cell with me. Will try, in future to keep a sealed bag in my car containing the books, and picture etc. I might want in custody. The coffee has sugar in but it is good. Now have an extra blanket so this is folded up at my back. Am told a special court hearing tomorrow, Bank Holiday. What a waste of public money.

To return to my night. My feet were very cold and I didn't like to ask for another blanket as I had two. Yellow wool and clean but old. The bench was 3ft wide. The mattress is 2 inch sorbo, plastic covered, so on top of this I put a blanket, fold my raincoat up and cover with pants to make a sort of pillow and cover with other thin blanket. Night-light is quite strong so difficult to sleep but I guess I do get some sleep. Ventilation comes up cold from under the "bed". Don't think it is extra cold but seems draughty and uncomfortable. Very noisy at times during night but this morning it sounds as if I am the only customer.

Things could be much worse. Just to think of the very dirty, badly lit cells of Witney, here I am in clover. My punishment for "crimes" I've committed. I think of my two Canadian friends in their early 20's who rescued 39 cats and will face severe punishments.

8.00 am. Would you like breakfast?", says another PC. Order taken.

8.15 am. Whistle, whistle and clatter of keys. "Here you are Cynthia, Breakfast" A plastic plate and two pieces of toast dripping with Flora. Ugh!! I never eat toast in the morning anyway and the greasy stuff will make me sick. I take the coffee and put in blue mug. "Don't you have a small cereal, Sir please"? "That is breakfast." Witney breakfast was better, seems to vary quality and quantity of food from clink to clink. I say I normally only have a small bowl of cereal and decline the greasy toast. I don't like to waste food but I was told "breakfast" and 2 pieces of bread and marg albeit toasted cannot honestly constitute a breakfast, or can it? Lucky I have half an apple left from last night (one I bought in.) Shouldn't grumble because in Witney breakfast didn't arrive until much later. The walls of cell 14 are emulsioned in a sort of hint of grey or green colour. Now to the graffiti that consists of some most interesting work.

"Paddy WOZ 'ere'... "In prison you get coffee, In prison you get tea, In prison you get everything, except the f****** key"... "F*** the police with a lump hammer"... "Quick it's the pigs"... "Don't be sad, don't be blue, I was arrested just like you." "Don't say anything 'cause life as a grass just won't do'... "Are you a hardcore raver or just a cheesy quaver, June 1992." ..."Give pigs no peace" ..."Pigs get more like slugs" ..."1992 Why don't the pigs answer the bells, you could die in here"..."Remember no f******comment 29.1.92 ALF" ..."Everything you say will be taken down in writing and used in evidence against you."

8.55 am. To my book. Oh yes, the loo here has a push flush. No paper so I use a bit of this type stuff.

9.00 am. Much screaming is heard. A drunk? A PC whistles.

9.05 am. Banging and a prisoner starts singing at the top of his voice.

9.10 am. WPC Sgt. introduces herself. I say breakfast NBG. She says she is trying to get my solicitor. She said she was reviewing my case. I ask her for some Gaviscon.[5]

9.42 am. Could do with my Gaviscon medicine. Guess she has forgotten. They don't sound busy. Don't want to ring the bell and be a nuisance again but really my request of 9.10 am should be granted.

9.55 am. Ring bell, solicitor on phone says, "get duty solicitor to help tomorrow."

---

5 A pain killer used in arthritis cases.

10.30 am. Someone, somewhere has made a mistake! Solicitor said they have never made a mistake. Always a first time and I'm stuck here. Could of course be worse. Now only 23 hours to wait. No offer of wash or comb and now 10.15 am. No Gaviscon arrives but tummy settles. Return to my book and rest neck on window ledge. Comfortable as can be. My German doctor in the book I'm reading is now practising obstetrics in the 1920's, before any antibiotics, so interesting.

10.40 am. Doesn't seem as if I'm expected to need a wash or brush for my hair or teeth.

11.10 am. My feet feel very cold again, icy cold. I lie down to get comfortable to read. Morning coffee would be nice; will I be offered any? I don't like to ask but will soon. My emergency police cell bag will contain a pair of warm socks. Perhaps gloves too. My hands are very cold. Sunshine gleams through the thick window glass. People go past. The sunshine makes the room nice and bright.

11.38 am. Any chance of a refill of coffee, please Sir?", "I should think so", as I hand him the blue china mug. Perhaps as dangerous as a pin badge but they allow me the mug. That will be nice. I strike out eleven on the clock chart I've designed on the wall. Wonder if Brendan will meet Neil. Expect Neil will phone Brendan when he doesn't arrive. I cannot understand why they did not arrest me earlier for this "crime". Still not offered any washing facilities. This cell is about 12ft by 8ft so I can walk up and down and around. Just paced it out.

12.00 noon. Coffee comes in plastic cup.

12.25 pm. Grub up. "It's a roast." I ask why they asked at 9.00 am if I wanted vegetarian. Carrots, two nice roast spuds and cauliflower and two slices of roast beef and gravy arrive. The food comes from the Church Army and it puzzles me that they cannot provide a veggie meal. Not too hot so I eat it quickly. The cow died, and to throw away, waste the meat offered, would I feel be very wrong although I haven't eaten such for months and wouldn't choose to. Guess one must not be fussy but it is 100% my right or supposed to be that I can have veggie food. A strawberry mousse follows. Did not really want to eat this but I hadn't had any breakfast bar half an apple and to waste food to me would be wrong. Gaviscon medicine comes. I had ordered at 9.15 am!

12.38 pm. Bang, bang, bang. Sounds like a new customer in. Have a siesta. Make the most of my enforced rest. Continue my very good book. This is the second time I am reading it. An officer comes. "Would you like to see your son?" I first have some Gaviscon. Brendan brings me in clean pants, hairbrush and clean dress and I return to the cell at 2.15 pm. An officer sits "listening in."

2.20 pm. Have the warm socks on. Someone is banging hard on cell door.

3.00 pm. Return to cell after a little exercise in yard about 36 x 12ft heavily security watched. Bit of blue sky but cold. At least the rain has kept off for the Cat's day. Tell PC I'd love a cup of coffee if one going. No view from exercise yard except 12 x 36 foot of sky space. I tick the hours by on my wall clock.

3.30 pm. In comes a cup of coffee, the *Independent* paper, chocolate and Ski yoghurt drink from Brendan. If he was here he would call. Nice to see the paper. Day is going by quickly.

4.45 pm. Solicitor from Cole and Hicks informs me how to behave tomorrow. Says they will give me bail.

5.20 pm. Plate of cheese salad and 2 bits of bread and Flora. I've been stuffing chocolate and just had the drink Brendan brought in. Can never eat salad cream. Ugh! This salad cream is over cheese and carrot mixture so eat cucumber, tomatoes, lettuce and a small piece of cheese. Must say food at Witney much better. Coffee is brought in. Only another 12 hours.

5.30 pm. A bit awkward sitting on this bed all day. Back only minimal trouble so I am lucky.

7.20 pm. Have been lying on one side to get comfortable to read. My hands feel very cold. Would have been difficult to put up with another full day like this. A chair with a back would be so very helpful. Am absorbed in my lovely instructive book. I glance at Molly.

10.30 pm. I ask for and get some more Gaviscon and a kind note from Neil. He has been waiting since 5.30 pm to 10.00 pm to see me. No room available!! Hard to really swallow that one. My feet are warm now. I'll try to sleep.

Bank Holiday Monday 31.8.92

1.50 am. Impossible to sleep. Some very noisy neighbours and the Pigs bang the doors to make as much noise as possible. At one stage I rang the bell as someone was banging the door so violently. I'm tired but doubt if I will get any sleep, as I was so inactive yesterday although reading. Bed too hard etc. Only another 6 hours now. Gosh it has been a long time and to think I am here 100% unlawfully.

2.14 am. Trying to get to sleep on my side and quite cold air is blown up from under the bed. Will try again to doze off.

5.15 am. "Noisy b******" I shout. Doors banging and doubt if I have slept at all. The lights are so strong and the noise! Prisoners bang and bang for attention (I know). One has started now. Wonder how long he will have wait. He could be ill but who really cares?

6.50 am. Wake with neck and backache. Must have had a little sleep as the noise calmed down. Sit with blanket around shoulders and full light is on as I've just called the Screw. "Could I have a wash please"? I haven't had one since admission." "I'm going off duty in 10 minutes, so if you could wait, otherwise they

have to pay me Bank Holiday rates." Guess it would be too much
to get a drink. Nice cop comes. "You can have a wash" and directs
me. After wash notice a shower. Have got Govt. soap, toothbrush,
comb, soap affair all in a towel. Try shower but only very luke
warm-cold so NBG. Feel better after the wash and here is coffee!

7.55 am. Lovely coffee.

7.10 am. Ring bell. I will make a written complaint re the Sgt. at
Banbury (S** to talk to me so threatening and rudely. I was not
too well). My eyes feel sore and tired but I could finish my book.
Will try to read now. There is no water tap in here so even to get
water, one has to beg!

7.22 am. Ring bell again. Guess they are all having a brew up.
Certainly do not sound busy. Makes the mind boggle how these
well paid officers refuse to do their job i.e. answer the bell.
Perhaps wash time is 7.30 and 7.30 only. I wasn't offered a wash
yesterday.

7.30 am. Nice cop comes who was on duty yesterday. "The problem is you have to be supervised having a wash." We will have
to get a WPC over from Cowley. I think this is a waste of police
time and what bad management not to have a WPC on duty with
a woman in the cells! They knew I was in and could have given
me washing facilities at 6.30am. It would not have worried me
and a WPC was on duty then. Said "a coffee, note paper and Code
of Practice are of more value to me than a wash please".

8.00 am. Locks me in again. Says they have trouble with the boi-
ler so no shower or hot water. I ask for a small bowl of cereal and
none available. Can't eat greasy toast so have to go without.
Coffee very nice. Am reading the Code of Conduct C86 P53 "at
least two light meals and one main meal shall be offered in any
period of 24 hours. As far as is practicable, meals provided shall
offer a varied diet and meet any special dietary needs or religious
beliefs that the person may have".

8.52 am. Minutes going by, have made a few notes for magistrates. Tidy my belongings. Court said to be for 9.30 so shouldn't be too long. Dreading they cancel and I am here another long day.

9.00 am. Ring bell. Figure 9 is crossed through on my wall chart. Ask about review procedure.

9.30 am. Keys clatter, clatter. I'm out. Can it be too much to ask for a drink of Nescafe? Which engineer designed the air vents under the bed? Only 2 more hours. Molly smiles. Of course the dogs and cats and monkeys and rats all know what we do for them. Should say "try". Wonder if Dr. could have obtained a pillow for me? Small pillow in my "take away bag". This is now my 3rd visit to cells so I should keep a bag ready. Can see daylight via the thick glass window chunks but don't know if it is sunny.

Expected to climb up quite a high step into the White Maria Prisoner's Van. A fellow prisoner gives me a good hand up. I'm asked to go into a minute cramped cell. "Have you no consideration. I do have a bad back." "You can sit in here if you like." Am given a seat at back and only 5 minutes ride. Two other prisoners are each locked in tiny cells.

9.42 am. Get out of van and in via prisoner's entrance and I am put into a cold, badly lit cell. I explain I may need medication and if I ring the bell would they come.

9.52 am. "Name please", I explain I have a water works problem and a bucket would be useful if I'm here for too long. Cell has dark red polished floor, dark green back and front walls (more difficult for graffiti artists) and cream walls to the sides. Both latter walls could do with a wash with Flash as s*** or sick on walls - or both. Very cold and will try to finish my book although light poor.

10.30 am. Very cold. "Did you ring the bell?" an officer calls. I say "no" and ask him the procedure. The Magistrates choose as they wish and there are a few of us. I say I've had no breakfast and the meal last night I could not eat. Guess I could be here 2 hours or more and it wouldn't surprise me if I'm last to be heard as I am particularly "a most nasty criminal." Screws go past. Gosh this is a nasty cold hole. Am still in custody. Is it too much to ask for a drink? Well wait a while. I'm very cold.

11.00 am. "Alright Cynthia"? I am told to go upstairs, "Isn't there a lift? Sure there is but they want to make it awkward. Past the police room and there must be WPC and four others smoking and drinking coffee. Would it have hurt them to offer all the prisoners coffee?

I enter the court and am told to "sit there." "Stand" comes from the Chair. "Please may I sit down I'm very cold and have a bad back and haven't had any breakfast? "Yes." No smiles. Thinks I have a nasty bit of work here. Prosecuting solicitor said her bit. Clerk asked me to speak. "A great miscarriage of justice etc." and I tell her that my solicitor phoned to say all cases had been dropped.

I'm given bail conditions, to sign on twice a week at local nick and attend court 9 Sept. What a sour lot. Still feel cold. Screw leads me out downstairs to police room and Sgt. seated, WPC and I think three other PCs in their rooms smoking and one close to me sitting down. No chair available. A lady next to room, who I think was CID, was seated and I ask for chair saying I'm not too good. As I hand my court paper to Sgt. I say, "Could I have a coffee please as I'm still in custody." "There is animal fat in so you won't want any." "It's not for you to say this and there is no excuse for you sarcasm." Is there a coffee machine or phone here please?" In no uncertain words I'm given instructions to a phone box. I need to get a bus home or phone Brendan. I am on two sticks and a 10p phone call could have been in order and a coffee or tea the least considering the cold cells. Leaving the court I get to the phone box.

Earlier I had requested that Sgt. makes a note that I asked for coffee as I was still in custody and I was refused. Must have been lucky to have my case heard before others. Got to phone box about 11.40. Felt a little unsteady, dazed, very cold and not too well crossing the road. I wait on bench for Brendan, my son to come and pick me up. I wonder at the callousness of man to man.

Like many campaigners before her, Cynthia felt drawn into the vortex of complaints and protest against the system as it increasingly came to bear on her. After her first detention she complained to CAB, and wrote to her MP informing him of appalling conditions. "No one cares a damn. The prisoners do not deserve such dreadful treatment."

1.9.92. Call to Witney station 5.00 pm to book appointment re complaint via Inspector. "Don't know his appointments. Phone 9.00 am tomorrow."

2.9.92. Phone 9.02 am. Ring, ring, ring for 3 minutes. Phone 9.05. "I'm busy all day then three weeks holiday. I'll phone you back", he says. I explain I should like to make a complaint today and have a friend coming over purposely.

Of course all the proper channels of complaint were pursued including Police Complaints Authority. What a waste of paper and a waste of time. However I was learning. They knew I was going to be a tough nut to crack!

Chapter Three

 **Proper Channels II**

Money to pay my first fine of £200 in 1992 was raised by the sale of my nursing badges and medal. What use were these treasured items, however hard earned, when every six seconds an animal was dying in a British Lab? That first hefty, cooked-up fine, however, did not deter me, only made me work harder![1]

In mid 1992, Hill Grove farm's trade in cats and holiday homes was only interrupted by the one or two protesters who stood regularly some way from the property with megaphones, sheets and hand-made placards.

As Cynthia's knowledge about vivisection grew, her campaign came to involve the very organisations that she had once believed protected animals. And she broadened her interests to include the pharmaceutical companies and the Cancer Research Charities which rely heavily on animals to test drugs.

When the Queen visited Glaxo in Stevenage in August 1992, to open a huge new research lab, Cynthia and a new acquaintance, the Rev. James Thompson, both aired their views on Cynthia's newly acquired megaphone.

To ensure that she arrived in good time, and in view of the long journey, Cynthia stayed overnight in a local hotel. Was she surprised when a notice informing her of the Queen's visit to Glaxo and the Fraud of Vivisection appeared under the bedroom

---

1 Cynthia O'Neill.

door? It's unlikely. She was, however, surprised by the hotel manager's evident consternation. The notice which *he* delivered apologised to hotel guests for the disturbing notices that had been distributed. Oh well, Cynthia sighed, "No peace for the wicked!"

On June 27th, 1992 an all night vigil was held at Martyr's Memorial in Oxford, especially to remember and draw attention to animals which had died in Oxford laboratories. To spread the message even further afield Cynthia felt justified in storming Oxfordshire Area Health Authority meetings on more than one occasion.

The AHA found their meetings interrupted by a woman in her fifties supported by walking sticks, shouting and awkwardly carrying a large home-made placard, "Stop vivisection in our hospital. A hospital is for sick people not the abuse of animals. Vivisection must be abolished." And "Close these hospital vivisection labs now". Security staff and large numbers of police officers were soon on hand at meetings to throw Cynthia out and stop the awkward matter of vivisection in Oxford hospitals from being discussed.

Cynthia made frequent visits to Prof. Blakemore's workplace, in Oxford University. Always she asked for a meeting with him, only to be told "He's at a meeting", "Gone abroad for a few days", "Not in the building" or "Not available."

> It was my concern to enquire as to what Prof. Blakemore and his staff do to these cats. A quick walk around the back of the buildings and even the litter bins tell many a tale. Empty animal cages of various sizes only need an ounce of common sense to put two and two together. Peculiar to see empty monkey cages outside the Dept. of Human Anatomy. Most odd!

Cynthia and her group confirmed that Hill Grove cats were sold to Oxford University, having followed a van making a delivery from the Farm to the University.

Cynthia's 'suss out' visits to Park Farm, University of Oxford's grounds for holding a variety of animals including dogs and a large number of monkeys, were becoming awkward. It was hidden from the public down a country road, and most people had no idea about the many petrified monkeys and other animals awaiting transport to the labs. Sometimes Cynthia would see boxes of bananas piled up high next to the monkey house. Her visits unnerved the staff and the administration and whenever she was spotted, a loud speaker system blarred "ALF alert, ALF alert."

Her jaunts also took her into the various departments of Oxford University. Physiology and psychology labs were notorious for most horrific experiments. All too often Cynthia was caught on the CCTV, easily recognisable on two walking sticks. Each time she visited there was a major alert and even sometimes a bomb search.   ·

Challenging the RSPCA[2]

As a member of the RSPCA one has certain privileges, to speak and address the Annual General Meeting (AGM) for example. In 1994, this AGM was held at Church House, London. It was an effort for Cynthia to get to London, difficult parking and hard to get around using her sticks. Nevertheless, Cynthia decided to put a motion at the AGM. A motion had to be properly seconded, signed and settled by a fixed date. The first paper Cynthia sent was returned due to a minor mistake, only a terrific rush and Registered Post got the motion received in time.

Her motion was eventually accepted in a letter received in 1994. Cynthia's speech made it clear why she thought that Hill Grove farm was a matter for the RSPCA.

---

2 In 1985, *The Guardian* reported that the RSPCA (Royal Society for the Prevention of Cruelty to Animals) had voted to expel one of its most radical members [*The Guardian* 30th May 1985]. Mr. Kim Stallwood, campaign organiser of the British Union for the Abolition of Vivisection, was voted off the council by a two-thirds majority. Stallwood had made himself unpopular with his RSPCA colleagues in January when he told a public meeting in Birmingham that the charity's Advisory Committee on Animal Experiments included practising experimenters. In June 1985, a stormy RSPCA AGM rejected both the accounts and report, and heard calls for the expulsion of four members of the society's Animal Experimentation Advisory Committee and demanded that Mr. Kim Stallwood be reinstated.

Cruelties permitted by British law in vivisection labs far out-weigh the worst cruelty cases ever seen by RSPCA Inspectors and it is a proven and well documented fact that these experiments are a medical and scientific fraud.

Over 300 million animals worldwide each year die in research labs. Innocent animals are blinded, burned, scalded, turned into drug addicts, poisoned to death, mutilated, dissected, starved, crippled, kept in solitary confinement, electric shocked, irradiated, frozen and otherwise tortured to death in the most shameful fraud in the history of the human race. This must not continue. The RSPCA must act now. Every 6 seconds an animal dies in a British lab, often death coming as a merciful release.

Modern medicine is based on theft and murder. Stolen pet animals, of which there is proof, are murdered in the name of medical research. To remain silent signifies acceptance. To remain silent is to lie and to accept these horrendous crimes.

With £75,000,000 invested, the RSPCA could spend a small fraction of their money informing the public and their members, of the cruelties: barbaric cruelties to animals, carried out in our schools, hospitals, universities, pharmacology labs and military research hell holes such as Porton Down.

This book of the truth (holding up *Slaughter of the Innocent*) should be sent free to every member of the RSPCA and all public libraries in the country. You would still have plenty in reserve. Money is given to the RSPCA to abolish cruelty, not to invest in stocks and shares! TV adverts must show the scandal of the greatest fraud of all time. Lab animals cry to you members of the richest animal welfare organisation. Do you speak up against the horrors of vivisection? ...No!

On behalf of the lab animals that cannot speak, I urge the Council to accept my motion and act without delay. All campaigns cost money, the RSPCA has money. RSPCA has plenty of money given to prevent cruelty to animals.

This motion for the animals demands action to abolish vivisection and therefore to stop cruelty... No good will ever come from evil.[3]

---

3 Part of text of Cynthia's talk drew upon information from Bette Overell of NZAVS (New Zealand Anti-Vivisection Society) , and literature supplied by Anne Phair.

Cynthia's speech was greeted with a roar of applause and amongst some, a standing ovation. Angela Walder seconded the motion, speaking excellently Cynthia thought. The vote went massively in Cynthia's favour: 146 votes, to 9 with 20 abstentions.

Cynthia heard later that four council members voted against the motion. And she was sanguine about its ultimate effect. Six years later, she said: "What has been done to support a fully passed RSPCA member's motion voted with a large majority? One guess. Exactly, nil." Another proper channel was due to fail.

I refer to my letter of 6.7.94 in response and correction to letter earlier. Three times I have phoned, 2nd, 5th & 10th August, requesting the courtesy of a reply at least. Why the silence? My motion was passed with terrific support on the 25th June.

You do have the funds to reply to letters and the monies available (£75,000,000) to spend a fraction on the motion that was passed at the AGM by members.

I should like a reply to my letter albeit an awkward letter for you to answer. As a member I am entitled to know why members cannot attend Council meetings as observers. Perhaps the Council have not met since the AGM?

I ask again, "What steps are the council to take re. abolition of Vivisection?" I asked for books e.g. "Slaughter of the Innocent" to be given to all RSPCA members and every library.

I request a reply please. Thank you. Remember that every six seconds an animal dies in a British lab. We must act now.[4]

The RSPCA remained unmoved:

Thank you for your letter dated 27th October 1994.

I am quite satisfied with the responses already given to your various questions and I therefore intend to take no further action.[5]

Birds of a feather

Having made a start stirring up the large societies, Cynthia's next port of call was the Cats Protection League (CPL).

---

4 Cynthia to the RSPCA. August 10, 1994.
5 R. F. Kirby, Chairman of RSPCA Council. November 14, 1994.

On the 1st Oct. 1994, again in London, Cynthia addressed the CPL AGM. Every day cats were leaving Hill Grove for the labs. Outside Hill Grove demonstrating alone or with a few others, Cynthia felt isolated. Cynthia figured that many more would hear of the campaign through her address to these Annual General Meetings.

Before the CPL AGM, Cynthia put leaflets on all the chairs. Surprisingly, these Anti-vivisection leaflets were soon scooped up by a committee member. Cynthia's well prepared four minute speech was spoken almost from memory while looking hard in the eyes of the perturbed committee.

Good afternoon Mr Chairman, Ladies and Gentlemen.

"If I had to justify my work in terms of clinical benefit before I started I would never have been given a licence", so said Prof. Blakemore of Oxford University.

The Journal of Neuroscience 1987 from which I quote says: "Cats were trained to walk on a horizontal walkway, which had moveable rungs to interrupt the cat's normal walking pattern. A deliberately uncomfortable "safety net" below the ladder prevented the cats from escaping. The cats had electrodes implanted in the brain and secured to the skull with acrylic cement. Recordings were made of brain activity during session on the apparatus." We should make recordings of the scientists' brains if any! This evil crime was paid for by a charity... Action Research U.K.

Another Charity that uses cats in their phoney experiments is the British Heart Foundation (BHF). Leeds University used 14 cats to investigate the distribution of certain substances in the brain. Under anaesthesia the animal's blood was drained and replaced with fixative. Their brains were then removed and examined. How does such a vile procedure help in the cure of heart disease? It is plain nonsense and they know it!

Bristol and Newcastle Universities too are blackspots for the cats. Another medical journal says: "cats were operated on. Their chests opened, part of the ribs and lung removed, and various nerves exposed and cut. A chemical tracer was applied to the cut nerves every two hours, to be taken to the brain. Anaesthesia was maintained for twenty four to twenty six hours. The cats were later killed and their brains removed." More charity funding by BHF. What a waste of money.

Innocent kittens were raised in a special chamber, so as to expose them to a long term lack of oxygen, and their breathing responses investigated. Later, they were found to have failed to develop normal responses to atmospheric oxygen. They also gained less weight than normally reared kittens. The Foundation for the Study of Infant Deaths and Action Research paid for this one. Did this wicked experiment tell the researchers anything new and how does a cat behave like an infant? As far as I know, infant cats do not die suddenly. That was a sample of Sheffield University's talent!

Where do these cats come from? In a little village near Oxford farmer Brown has 1,000 cats for sale to the labs. But stolen cats also find their way into the labs from all over the country... cats are easy to pick up and are much favoured as lab tools, as their brains are so sensitive.

Are we a nation of animal lovers that remain silent to these disgraceful, disgusting and shameful crimes?

The CPL *Caring for Cats*, page 8 & 9, states the Protection of Animals Act 1911 saying that any one who infuriates, terrifies or tortures an animal can be prosecuted. If this law was exercised then the prisons would be full of vivisectors. Painful experiments are carried out, very painful because giving analgesia would invalidate any results. Cats are fully immobilised in stereotaxic devices and experimented on. But the laws are for vivisectors, the 1986 Act is a vivisector's charter. Cats are infuriated, terrified and tortured every second of the day in this country, as the majority of those in power who should speak out, remain silent.

As with Cynthia's motion at the RSPCA AGM, her resolution that immediate steps were taken by the CPL to abolish vivisection was passed by a large majority. Unlike the RSPCA meeting, however, the Committee of the CPL let their feelings for Cynthia's cause be known by failing to detail the motion in the summing up at the end of the meeting. There followed a great furore, with Cynthia on her feet shouting at the committee and accusing them of various things. During the row, the meeting was closed for five minutes so that order could be restored. It was clear that the CPL did not want to embrace the anti-vivisection cause and quoted its "non political" charity status to support its position. After the meeting, Cynthia was again terribly disappointed that the CPL did nothing to implement her motion.

Some time later, when Cynthia's membership was terminated by the CPL, she travelled to the Horsham HQ with a friend to state her case. Cynthia asked point blank if the CPL had interests in any pharmaceutical companies; she was told, "It's none of your business." "At least", Cynthia said, "one can honestly say that I tried the proper channels."

Throughout all these interventions, and as the picket of Hill Grove farm continued, Cynthia was still raising money. Money from the stalls paid for a large double-sided cloth banners. 'Vivisection is Scientific Fraud', it said on one side. Sticky labels and many leaflets and postcards with the same slogan came from collecting tins known as the begging bowls. Indeed when she attended car boot sales, having paid her £5 rent, Cynthia did sometimes actually beg: "I was allowed to beg 'Have you a spare penny please?'" as she handed out leaflets. Spare pennies were often pounds and even sometimes a £5 note. "If you don't ask you don't get!", she would say. Sometimes when it was very cold Cynthia would return home crying with the pain in her back.

Cynthia's next port of call was the British Union of Anti Vivisection (BUAV). She had attended the 1992 BUAV AGM and she organised for the event in 1994.

In 1994, the Annual General Meeting was a rumbustuous affair. The BUAV was at the very centre of the chaotic in-fighting between factions of the Anti-Vivivisection and animal liberation movements. As in many similar faction fights, the lines were relatively clearly drawn, between those who wanted a speedy and absolute end to vivisection and those who in various shades thought that eventual abolition could be achieved one step at a time.

Cynthia was immediately embroiled in these altercations, steadfastly on the side of an immediate end to vivisection. This was the strategy she was adopting to Brown's Farm; this was who Cynthia was. Her notes of the 1994 General Meeting give a good impression of the internecine fight which was going on inside the movement.

Six times prior to the meeting I phoned, making every effort to get my comments raised. "You will just have to come and fill in a speaker's slip from 11.00 am." They were not interested in the problems of my ninety mile journey and the difficulties caused by my disability. BUAV had not bothered to secure a meeting venue with parking for the disabled and because it would be a struggle with a car I left home at 6.15 am to get three buses and then a taxi to reach the Central Hall, Westminster for 9.30 am.

Not being a good traveller, on the coach into Oxford I felt quite unwell, but on the larger Oxford Tube, as it is known, which goes almost non-stop by bus to London, I was soon off to sleep. The book *Dirty Medicine* which I had started to read, slept with me. My intention was to get to the venue early and use our megaphone. Use it I did, I ended up with two police warnings instigated by the BUAV! There was great embarrassment at what I was saying to the members as they went in. Demanding to know where the money goes, etc.

Even before the meeting began, late, Ralph was asking for the Chair to resign. Heated protests, and from the Chair: "Do you want me to throw you out Ralph?" I had handed in a slip to question the accounts but I doubted selection. I was proved wrong as my turn came to address the 450 or so members plus officials and staff.

Many of us kept heckling but when it came to Rover cars as being cheap for BUAV staff, I was flaming, but I did get my turn. I said that such large salaries amount to theft from the animals... Money! Rover cars! If anyone did their work they would be worth paying. I mentioned Francis Cobbe, the founder to much applause and her aims for total abolition, none of this 10% nonsense. I was quite polite in the circumstances. "If BUAV had been doing the work they are paid for, these filthy crimes of vivisection would have been abolished years ago!" (applause).

During the meeting, the BUAV Committee were shown up and enough good people had cared to join for this one reason i.e. to get a new Committee elected and so get vivisection abolished.

Candidates for election spoke and the first, Louise O'Gara asked for one minute's silence for lab animals. The Hall was hushed in prayer. Why hadn't BUAV ask for this gesture? Helen Alexander was asked some heated questions re direct action and she got plenty in return. "Even to save one lab animal in a raid is worthwhile", I shouted, others applauded loudly.

It was a very hot day and we were all getting tired. Yet the candidates continued and lunch break was not until 2.40 pm. Luckily I had brought my own sustenance, but in view of the long journeys many had made a break should have been made as planned for approximately 1.30 pm. Another example of incompetence.

To get to the Café in Westminster Hall, one had to go down three flights of stairs and there were no lifts. The afternoon proceedings were equally shameful, in fact very shameful. From the start of the meeting I had been out several times to phone a news reporter who of course was not allowed to attend.

To say the meeting was dragged out is no exaggeration. Voting for Resolutions was only on slips and it was suggested we all exchange papers. No real secrecy at all! Good and true people spoke and then my turn came. I had heard a few of the other speeches like that of Patrick Rattigan, they gave me heart.

For Resolution 7.2.2 I had my full four minutes. My theme was theft of the money meant for the animals. "Do you think the branch would get permission to use £500 for a lab raid and rescue. Of course not! That is why HQ want to keep the money". "Bolton branch could spend the money on Ruesch's books to go to every library in the country if they wish. They are the trustees of this gift." A hint was also dropped for ARTL. I had to accuse anyone failing to support this resolution as being guilty of theft. "Animals are dying in torture a stone's throw from here as you sit on other people's money." My humble efforts for the animals were well applauded and the motion was accepted with few against.

Some members standing for re-election had previously worked for BUAV and were not happy with things, such as money wasted on legal fees and, allegedly, handouts to a person who already had a well paid job to go to. The muddle seemed to be total and it had to be stopped.

Very red faces showed and heated exchanges took place when a copy of eight allegedly forged BUAV staff signatures appeared on a very important document and the term "Oh, he is one of us" was used. We abolitionists know who "one of us" refers to. Those who do not want the complete and immediate abolition our Founder of 96 years ago sought.

In 1994, Cynthia also took on the Wellcome Trust. The Trust, originally founded on profits from the Wellcome Foundation drug company, has become the biggest medical research funder in Britain. Its vast offices support a library, a museum, a department of University of London as well as hundreds of researchers in hospitals and laboratories throughout the country.

Cynthia came across a notice for a Study Day entitled, *Animal models, an historic perspective*. Fellow activists were alerted. Again, Cynthia's account is entertaining.

Indeed it was a most foul meeting. Dressed as what one was, a State Registered Nurse interested in medical history, I made the long journey to London and did the difficult walk on two sticks from the Euston railway station.

I wore nothing to give the game away and my 20p car boot sale imitation pearl necklace looked exactly the part. I was to be most lady-like, or try to be, and keep my trap shut until the right opportunity and then let go. Having been careful to remove any anti-vivisection badges I normally had about my person, I signed in, collected my name badge, sat in the very plush foyer listening and observing.

To think that out of all the thousands that could attend, only one lone anti-vivisectionist went for the lab animals. I found that Disgraceful! The name badges I saw were most entertaining, two individuals at least were from BUAV.

By ten that morning I knew I was going to get my money's worth. Famous vivisectors would be talking about the great 'benefits' to mankind of their work. Frog research sounded especially stupid. A heart research vivisector who uses umpteen rats gave his report.

How I kept from shouting out I don't know, especially when one vivisector described the direct breaking of an animal's bones to give a fracture. I knew that I simply had to listen to these filthy lectures and watch the equally horrific slides and films until my chance came.

Going to lunch, mixing with vivisectors and others who hadn't cottoned on to my function and "criminal record", was both sickening and amusing. Half way through lunch I realised there was support, the noise began outside. Lovely stuff. Drums, whistles and a megaphone gave gorgeous background.

I sneaked out during lunch to see my friends and congratulate them. "Lovely job! Louder please, keep it up." The drummer was delighted that his drumming was so very effective. Questions and answers concluded the seminar and I gave one of my best performances. I felt a little lonely but imparted good solid home truths.

I was escorted from the building by two security staff to join the even noisier shouting and drumming. For some reason my name was struck off the Wellcome Trust mailing list. My membership of a number of organisations was running out and my chance to storm the citadel of Proper Channels gradually diminishing. I did try, however.

Shirley's Story

My name is Shirley, I first met Cynthia O'Neill when I was visiting England with my husband Len in 1993. She had a table set up in the street in Stow-On-The-Wold. She was giving out literature and talking to the general public on the useless and cruel practice of vivisection. Len and I have been involved in animal welfare for many years in Australia. We were drawn to Cynthia like moths to a flame -we all know what animal lovers are like. I have always felt in my heart that vivisection is a vile and evil thing and even thinking about it raises my worst nightmare.

After talking to Cynthia for some time, happily finding that we had so many thoughts in common, she invited us both for a meal with her that night. She asked where we were staying, and when I said that we were hunting for a B&B somewhere, Cynthia replied by asking if we would like to stay with her. We could also take the opportunity to speak about anti-vivisection. I believe so strongly in fate, and that some things are just meant to be. Meeting Cynthia was one of those things.

At the time we took this holiday to the U.K., I was well and truly in need of a break from all the heartache that happens to people who do not shut their eyes to the neglect, cruelty and suffering meted out by society to voiceless animals. I had been rescuing surviving stray cats from the streets, graveyards, docklands, building sites and, sadly, households of Melbourne.

I was thankful for the holiday, thinking it would confirm my belief that the English were a land of animal lovers. Though as so often happens in life, some of my illusions crumbled and disappointment took their place when I heard about the Hill Grove cats.

Fate had brought me from Melbourne to meet Cynthia in England, a remarkable woman, who at this time had taken up the campaign to close the breeder down almost single handed. How awful, that the farmer who ran this 'business' was at the same time running a guesthouse. The people who paid him money to sleep in his beds were not aware that down the back were sheds containing imprisoned cats.

Even in primary school science we are taught as children that to get a correct result in an experiment, you must compare like with like. You cannot experiment on making house paint by painting a cardboard box and putting it in the weather to see what happens, you must paint a house. You cannot experiment on human medicines and expect a proper result if you test on anything other than a human. Anything other than this, is absolute nonsense.

Why is there so much more human cancer than ever before? Could one of the contributing factors be that there are more chemicals, preservatives, colouring, etc. in our food? Some of which have been tested on animals. Have these cruel tests proved anything? Is there any justification, scientific or moral, that can explain pouring shampoo into the unprotected eye of an animal? Can there possibly be any justification either scientific or moral, for the breeding of live creatures that feel fear and pain, to sell their little bodies to laboratories?

All holidays must end and Len and I returned home. Cynthia kept us up to date with her campaign to close this dreadful business down. Thank God for her determination and tenacity, she gathered a group of lovely people who all felt the same way.

The war will not be won until humanity takes a moral stance and universally outlaws vivisection and any products associated with this practice. Thank God for Cynthia O'Neill. The world needs people like her that respect and love the wonderful animals who share our world.

Shirley

Chapter Four

🐈 The Consequences of Actions

As man proceeds towards his announced goal of the conquest of nature, he has written a depressing record of destruction, directed not only against the earth he inhabits but against the life that shares it with him.[1]

Inevitably, more radical action usually accompanies pursuit of a campaign through 'proper channels.' It didn't take Cynthia long to realise that she had to act as well as write letters and attend meetings. By the summer of 1992, she was involved with others in discussing raids and demonstrations against vivisectors and their animal breeding establishments in the Oxfordshire area.

Hearing the beagle dogs in Park Farm and seeing the conditions in which they were kept prompted three activists to try to liberate them. No bedding, no heating of any description, no toys and no love. Cold concrete kennels that Cynthia had observed on a number of occasions. One rescued dog was put in a safe house, but due to infiltration he was found quickly by the police and his freedom ended. When the police arrived, the new owner had a cheque in her hands for £2,000 to buy 'Jeremy', despite this and the fact that the market price for a beagle lab dog was £400, the dog was returned to it's hell.

The raid, although ultimately unsuccessful, made newspaper and TV stories and inevitably spread the word about vivisection in Oxford. After the recapture of Jeremy, Cynthia was arrested

---

1 Rachel Carson. *Silent Spring*. Penguin Books, Harmondsworth England. 1965.

along with a number of other activists. With charges of theft and burglary levelled at her, Cynthia opted for trial by jury. Before she could begin to work on her defence, however, all the charges were dropped. She took this as a sign of her growing strength and the authorities fear of attacking her in a public arena. Evidently, Park Farm did not want to wash its dirty linen in public yet again.

Re: Yourself: Witney Magistrates Court 17ᵗʰ Aug.1992.

I write to give you notice under Section 23(3) Prosecution of Offences Act 1985, that I have served notice on the Magistrates Clerk that I do not want the proceedings listed below to continue against you.

On 19ᵗʰ April, 1992 at Northmoor with others you entered as a tres-passer Park Farm and stole therein two Beagle Dogs of a value of £800 Contrary to Section 9(1) of the Theft Act 1968.[2]

The Chancellors, Masters and Scholars of the University of Oxford were not so concerned about their liberal image, they took out a High Court injunction against Cynthia, the first of many, to stop her getting near Park Farm again.

The High Court Injunction was brought by Oxford University on October 22ⁿᵈ 1992. Sadly, Cynthia reflected, she was a lone victim. If twenty or thirty like-minded activists collected injunctions then perhaps Oxford University would worry about the cost of injunctions. Cynthia took pride, however, in the knowledge that she was just one in a long line of people who had acted against Park Farm over the last ten years.

Almost a decade before, in July 1985, eight hundred people from Britain and Europe had gathered outside the holding area. This peaceful protest, policed by over 40 officers, was the sequel to two Animal Liberation League raids on the premises earlier in the month, when over thirty dogs had been released. The demonstration organisers charged the University of Oxford with holding animals which would certainly be put to death in experiments, they also accused the farm of holding domestic pets which had been stolen and sold to the farm. Activists went on to demonstrate outside Witney police station where they demanded that the police investigate the theft of animals. The officer in charge, at

---

2 Crown Prosecution Service. August 4, 1992.

the time, Cyril Williams, was not prepared to comment. He was presented with 500 protest letters handed in outside the police station, calling on the police to answer questions about their dealings with Park Farm.[3]

Hill Grove farm was visited again by the ALF on April 8th 1992. Brown's secure alarm system foiled the liberation of any cats. However, the unsuccessful raid made the Browns aware of the ALF's future intentions.

Late one night in early 1993 two activists tried to effect a small symbolic rescue. They too were foiled by the the alarm system. These two activists later told Cynthia that the noise of the hundreds of cats was terrible. At least they had done some damage while on the farm, which would put the owner to some trouble. It was, said Cynthia 'economic sabotage' and suggested that "At least they had tried. Better to try and fail than not bother at all!"

By now house raids by the police were quite common occurrences in the Oxford area. Everything in the house would be turned over including mattresses and carpets! Cynthia was frequently raided. Her major way of raising money for the cause, the stall in Oxford, was now regularly disrupted by the police. She played a game of cat and mouse for a while, moving the whole stall on to another place until she was moved on again.

A letter from France

A few years ago, I received a card from England: *"Hi Hans, I have seen your anti-vivisection article, great. Thank you. I am fighting it also. Cynthia."* Somehow - without knowing why - I felt that there was a strong personality behind these lines. I informed Cynthia about what had happened to me a few days prior: I had driven to Nimes in the South of France, to attend an *anti-corrida*[4] demonstration. I had a banner made up in the form of a giant cross, covered with

---

3 *Witney Gazette*, August 1, 1985.

bull-fight scenes and photographs of Jean Cadilhac, the Archbishop of Nimes, a corrida-fanatic, who spent more time in the arenas than in church. But the organisers excluded me from the demonstration - because of the cross, so I decided to carry it alone for 3 hours through the city of Nimes.

Cynthia was most impressed. She wrote to me: "*Last Sunday, I walked into a crowded church and asked the worshippers to pray with me for the Hill Grove cats!*" It was my turn to be impressed. Let's face it, it takes some nerve to interrupt a church service and start to pray alone, in a loud voice, for the poor creatures of God. The priests never do! Except for one it seems, the one and only Rev. James Thompson, known and admired as our "Animal Padre". He was not afraid to travel to Hill Grove and pray with Cynthia and a growing number of animal protectors, for the cats inside the breeding centre - born only to be tortured to death!

I am proud to say that the Animal Padre called me a friend! And this is due to the wonderful Vesna Jones, the courageous founder of the Greek Animal Rescue. She established contact by sending me Rev. Thompson's outstanding book: *Cast out of the Ark*. Give me a Cynthia O'Neill and a clergyman like Rev. Thompson in each country and the vivisectors would be on the dole!

Besides Vesna, a great number of other English ladies have written to me about Hill Grove, forwarding bits and pieces of information and encouraging me to write articles: Amanda, Diane, Jill, Hannelore, Phyllis, Jackie... the list is endless. A big thank you to all of them! After Cynthia sent a few cassettes of stormy conversations between her and the cat breeder's wife, Katherine Brown, I felt I should try to drum up some support for her.

I asked her to forward a few facts on her Hill Grove engagement, to enable me to write about her struggle, 15

---

4 The anti-bull fighting movement in France and Spain.

pages of hand written information arrived. I was a happy man; my Hill Grove articles have been published in animal magazines all over Europe. Support in the form of donations, used stamps and signature lists started to reach Cynthia.

I knew all the time that Cynthia would not give up. I knew that she would succeed, her charming British stubbornness would end cat breeding at Hill Grove farm. I was looking forward to this day, praying for it, living for it.

Hans Fischinger

Hurd gets a bit of megaphone diplomacy

Animal rights campaigner Cynthia O'Neill had a brief encounter with Witney MP Douglas Hurd when she turned up for his constituency advice clinic in Bampton. Ms O'Neill, 57, of Church Meadow, Milton-Under-Wychwood, says Mr Hurd has been refusing to meet her for two years. So, on Saturday morning, equipped with a megaphone, placard and leaflets, she lay in wait for the former Foreign Secretary at Bampton Town Hall. "I had a megaphone, so he heard me whether he liked it or not, but the police told me to 'shut it', because I was disturbing him", she said. "Vivisection is a money making fraud. He won't talk about it because there is too much money in it. I saw him three years ago but since then he has refused to see me and talk about vivisection. He keeps fobbing me off." Mr Barry Norton, Mr Hurd's constituency agent, said the MP spoke to Ms O'Neill briefly before going into the town hall. "He didn't ignore her. He went over and said a few private words to her. After a few moments he went inside and carried on with his surgery," he said. Mr Norton added that after about an hour Ms O'Neill gathered her possessions and left quietly to continue with the fight against vivisection…

"A new friend had joined me and we went in to see Douglas Hurd and kept him answering difficult questions." To get an interview she told a white lie giving the subject she wanted to discuss as Landlord and tenant. Had she said Hill Grove farm, there of course would be "no appointments left!"

Oxford Mail, February 19, 1996

Chapter Five

🐈 An Angel in Jeans

The word 'impossible' is not in my dictionary![1]

Cynthia's has a lot to say about the day to day frustration of organising campaigns, of the real difficulties of building a mass
movement. The constant letter writing, appeals for help and begging for small donations, Cynthia learned all this herself over a
period of four years at the beginning of her campaign. She experienced constant small set backs but they never put her off, she
learned from them.

> It was such a hard job to get any helpers. A new friend I'd meet
> on a stall would promise to meet 6.45am at Witney for a car boot
> sale. Not too early for a boot sale. The usual excuses we all
> know: "Don't feel well," "my parents are coming over," "over-
> slept", and so on. In other words 99% of it is "I really couldn't
> care, you'll never change things." What if the anti-slave trade
> campaigners and Suffragettes had said that? The imprisoned Hill
> Grove cats were constantly on my mind, if only in the form of a
> question "We will win one day - but how?"

More than anything, Cynthia had the sense and the humility to
understand that even the smallest contribution is of value and
those who make it worthy of respect. She gives this account of
her first meeting with one of the campaign's most valuable activists.

---

1 Cynthia O'Neill

Amongst all these excuses and all the asking, amongst the embarrassment of having to be rejected by people who had more time for painting their finger nails than saving living creatures from torture, there always comes a surprise.

We continued going to the farm throughout February 1996. They were very cold mornings, but we went all the same. We carried our home-made placards and the megaphone. The *Witney Gazette* gave us a front-page colour splash; weekly publicity was a must.

The new megaphone we needed cost a few pounds so an advert was placed in *Your Cat* magazine. A free advert, under Wanted, it read "All used postage stamps wanted please to help me raise funds to inform people of medical experiments using live cats. Thank you." My name, address and phone number were added.

A few replies came, one in particular from a Natasha in Worcestershire. The letter showed good handwriting, and a desire to help, so I suggested that we meet. We arranged a halfway rendezvous at the Little Chef at Stow-on-the-Wold on a cold Saturday morning. Snow had been falling quite heavily overnight. The roads were icy and snowflakes were still falling at nine that morning. The roads would have had to be impassable for me not to go. Would Natasha turn up? With voluntary work so many are just talk. Would Natasha really come with such bad roads?

I sat in the warmth of the Little Chef occasionally trying to picture her appearance while I happily wrote some of my many letters. Any gifts, however small, even a few used common stamps, were in my opinion worthy of a written reply and of course an opportunity to distribute a few leaflets. I've always written thank yous albeit some months late.

Despite the weather, Natasha arrived on time. A tall, thin, black haired, beautiful brown eyed twenty six year old woman dressed in jeans and a jacket. Her warm kind eyes said it all. How can I help? Wonderful Natasha, I call her an angel in jeans.

What a gem! What a find from a free ad in *Your Cat*. Didn't we do well! Didn't the Hill Grove cats do well? Explaining to her over a cup of coffee that she was in the company of a known criminal, I suggested that perhaps she may not like to associate with a criminal. "Show me your companions and I'll tell you what you are", she said gently. Very true. But it was only fair to tell my new friend that the price of our unpaid work could be very high indeed. Constant police harassment, phone tapping, wrongful arrests, court appearances and much more.

Today, four years since our first meeting, my angel in jeans has been locked up four times, served a prison sentence, been fined, pushed, shoved and assaulted by police and had CS gas delibe-rately sprayed in her face. She's been there as the struggle has continued. As the campaign transformed itself from a small group of marginalized activists to a campaigning army, Natasha has never faltered in her commitment.

Laura's story

The first time I went to Hill Grove there were four of us. On a very windy day, we stood on Burford Road with a huge banner. It was a cold day but our spirits were high. We were all there together for the same reason, to inform the public of the goings-on at the farm and to uncover the truth about animal experiments.

I couldn't believe Christopher Brown had been allow-ed to continue breeding cats for so many years with no one batting an eyelid. But now people were being told about Hill Grove and they were beginning to take an interest at last.

Demonstrations at the farm got bigger with people coming from all over the country and even further. Van loads of concerned people turned up with sleeping bags and stayed overnight. A camp was set up and eventually a huge campaign was underway.

I remember the atmosphere of people all joining to-gether to help the cats, the feeling of compassion amongst the protestors. Most were complete strangers but we were all involved in the same struggle, the struggle for the cats of Hill Grove.

Then there were times when I had felt so depressed knowing that there would be cats going to their deaths during the campaign. Feeling helpless but plodding on. If I stopped then so might others and what would happen to the cats then! We had to keep up the pressure. We had to show Brown that we would not tolerate his business. It wasn't all doom and gloom. I remember a cold looking farm labourer who arrived every morning on a small moped which looked like it belonged to a small child, its engine sounding like a burnt out hairdryer as he turned into the driveway. That always made me laugh.

Once a friend and myself were staying overnight and had a little drink to pass the time. We were listening to Radio 2 late at night and singing along at the top of our voices, verses from a Judy Garland song, through a megaphone. The police turned up several minutes later saying that Brown had complained of rowdy singing and if we didn't keep the noise down we would be arrested for being drunk and disorderly.

There was also the time that Brown came down his field while the camp was being set up. He got quite annoyed that we were on his land and he began leaning over me in a threatening manner and as he turned away, a dog from the camp, who evidently knew the score, leapt up and bit him on his backside. He wasn't too pleased as you can imagine, he stormed off mumbling something about his land.

Laura Brett

Cynthia O'Neill

Snowy, Cynthia O'Neill's cat stolen in September 1991 along with other cats in the area

Witney

Campaign picture

Natasha and Cynthia 'begging'

Campaign picture

Polite beginnings

Hill Grove
Farm

Campaign picture

A small mid-week afternoon protest

Oxford Courier Newspapers

THAMES VALLEY POLICE

SECTION 14
PUBLIC ORDER ACT 1986
IS IN FORCE REGARDING
ASSEMBLY LOCATION

PERSONS GOING
ONTO THIS LAND
ARE LIABLE TO ARREST

Describing boundaries

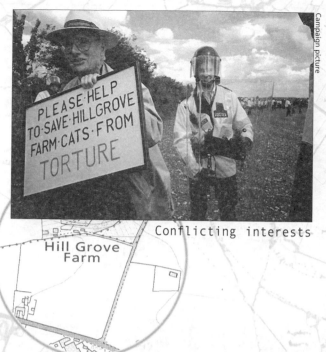

Campaign picture

Conflicting interests

Hill Grove
Farm

Campaign picture

A Scottish contingent

Dagmar,
Cynthia
and Roswitha

Campaign picture

Hill Grove
Farm

Laura and
Natasha
in action
at the
camp

Campaign picture

Campaign picture

Police about to arrest 94 year old Marion

Chapter Six

🐈 Christmas with a Difference

In Dulci Jubilio, we've come to see you ho, ho, ho. Come to tell you of your crimes...[1]

1996 turned out to be a very busy year for Cynthia and Natasha. It was Natasha who made the decision that the two of them should be more focused about their protest on Hill Grove farm; the more general campaigns against vivisection, even that against Oxford University Labs, should be put aside for the moment. News of the small group of determined protesters was spreading rapidly and at each demonstration and picket, Cynthia would entreat people to bring at least one other person to double the numbers at the next demonstration.

Natasha, who had been knocking on front doors with the group's Oxford University petition, always managed to gather recruits. Cynthia remembers her full of enthusiasm exclaiming about six new recruits for the Sunday morning picket. Battle weary, Cynthia inevitably wondered if they would come. As she stepped out of her car at Hill Grove that morning just opposite the entrance to Dry Lane on the main road, bathed in glorious sunshine, dressed in cool bright clothing and headed by Natasha, the small group came to join her, joyfully waving their hand-made placards.

---

1 Christmas carol aimed at vivisectors.

They had done it, a real demo! In Cynthia's mind that Sunday morning in early May 1996 marked their first real demo –twelve people. From that beginning, the Sunday morning demonstration and others began to grow. Most of their demonstration days seemed to be blessed with sunshine and on that beautiful May morning with Hill Grove birds singing there seemed to be magic in the air.

Cynthia performed one of her individual protests at the local Witney Job Centre, when she saw the following advertisement for Hill Grove farm.

```
     JOB CENTRE: MAN OR WOMAN
        JOB: Animal Attendant
     DISTRICT: Minster Lovell
  WAGE: At 18+ £120.00 plus bonus
     At 20+ £128.00 plus bonus

  HOURS: 8AM-4PM Monday to Friday
     5 hours overtime (Weekend)
 DETAILS: Person required to care for cats.
 Duties include grooming, feeding and playing
 with the cats. Animals are bred for research
 purposes. No research is done on site.
```

Cynthia removed the card from the board, tore it up in front of a long queue and then refused to move as the manager of the job centre called the police.

The annual Lab. Animals Day, on April 26 1996, was an auspicious day; the campaign organised its first big demonstration outside Hill Grove farm and the core activists founded their own anti-vivisection organisation, ACT-AV (The Active Campaign to Abolish Vivisection). One of the aims of ACT-AV was to keep the public informed by means of the local papers and the small group aimed for at least one letter or news item to be published each week. A business-like little group in the early days, ACT–AV soon had to suspend meetings because they were too busy!

The campaigners kept to their target of frequent news stories, usually by providing the newspapers with an incident, a demo or something personal to hang the story on. Later in the year, they began holding vigils at Oxford Martyr's Memorial.

VIGIL FOR THE ANIMALS

A group of anti-vivisectionist campaigners from across the area have held a second successful vigil at Oxford's Martyrs Memorial. The group is organised by Mrs Cynthia O'Neill from Milton-Under-Wychwood who said the vigil passed off peacefully on July 27th and that amongst those gathered were guests from as far away as Australia. Mrs O'Neill said the event was held in memory of the animals that would die in laboratories around the world that night as part of research carried out by medical bodies, the cosmetic industry and the military. "For one evening a month as dusk falls the animals are not alone," said Mrs O'Neill. Mrs O'Neill said the group was joined by supporters throughout the world who lit candles to mark the evening. Mrs O'Neill, who as reported in the *Standard* recently now collects tin cans from the streets to help fund the fight against animal experiments, feels that after years of campaigning people are beginning to realise why she does it. "People have got faith in me and are helping the cause by buying leaflets. But we still need money," said Mrs O'Neill. The next vigil will be held on August 24th, again in Oxford.[2]

Cynthia believed that the churches could do much if they wanted to. On more than one occasion Cynthia visited churches demanding that the congregation act as Christians. One local vicar invited Cynthia to his home, to talk not about the ending of vivisection, but about his annoyance at the messages entered in his visitors book. Prayers were often asked for 'vivisection to be abolished!' and the congregation were urged to 'pray for animal activists in prison today.'

---

2 *The Cotswold Standard,* August 6, 1996 (*The Cotswold Standard* later became *The Standard* and it is referred to by this name for the rest of this book).

A busy year came to its close with a special Christmas carol singing session for the Brown family. For some months Cynthia had been adapting appropriate words to well known Christmas carols. Christmas was no different for Cynthia than every other day of the year; she had the cats constantly on her mind.

What is Christmas to us, now we know of the dreadful crimes of vivisection? Every day is the same. Every day we hear the cries of the tortured cats. There can be no happiness for the true anti-vivisectionists. Glittering tinsel, pretty cards, fancy lights, deco- · ration for trees and churches, with by far the great majority of the parishioners oblivious to Hill Grove or vivisection, fill me with shame and sadness.

Anna, a well wisher, had made thirty six vegetarian mince pies. Armed with carol sheets, a map, tape recorder with recorded carols for background music and the, by now, well-used megaphone, five campaigners set off for Hill Grove farm where they got as close as they could to the cat sheds.

For the Browns they chose to sing *Silent Night*. When Brown came out to enquire about the racket they ended up having a recorded discussion. Brown's position had not changed, "What if your cat had cat flu. Vaccines from my cats would save yours." After a while Thames Valley police arrived and escorted the carol singers back to their cars. Their intelligence gathering was a little blatant says Cynthia; "Where next Cynthia?", asked one cop. Changing the subject, the warm mince pies were handed around.

"Bellamy next, follow me," said Cynthia to the other car drivers, Mr Bellamy being chief administrator of Oxford University. Careful to see that the police had gone they made their way to his home. For him and his household they sang a variety of carols and in between neighbours got to hear of vivisection at Oxford University. Over the megaphone the group sang: *As vivisectors watched with glee lab animals wracked in pain...* to the tune of *While Shepherds Watched*. The cops were quicker this time, itching to know the next target.

After more mince pies it was off to the final recipient of their Christmas message, Prof. Colin Blakemore. Making sure the police had left them, they arrived near his house; the residents were probably surprised to hear Christmas carols with a difference fill the air. Well, like it or lump it they weren't breaking any law by carol singing, albeit with peculiar words. *As vivisectors watched with glee...* More police arrived but they need not have worried, the demonstrators were tired and ready to go home.

Cynthia was to say later that it was one of her best Christmas Days.

Part Two

*A change of pace
and a counter offensive*

Chapter Seven

🐈 An Ugly Incident

The fight is nor for us, nor for our personal wants or needs. It is for every animal that has ever suffered and died in vivisection labs, and for every animal that will suffer and die in those same labs unless we end this evil business now. The soul of the tortured ones cry out for justice, the cry of the living is for freedom. We can create that justice and we can deliver that freedom.[1]

On January 18th 1997, Barrie Horne was on his first hunger strike. A vigil was organised outside the gates of Bullingdon Prison.[2] We drove up from Hove with a friend, her teenage daughter and their dog.[3] After the vigil the demonstration decided to move on to Harlan and then to Hill Grove farm. We had to meet someone at Oxford station so decided to find our way to Hill Grove by means of a map. We had never been there before so when we got to Dry Lane and saw the small signpost saying "Hill Grove" we followed the direction that pointed down a (unbeknown to us private) track.

At the end was a gate across the path. As I started to back the car out, a police officer appeared from behind the other side to the gate and beckoned us towards him. He approached our car and spoke to us through the open window.

---

1 Barry Horne, September 1998.
2 In early 1997, members of ACT-AV had been to a very cold vigil outside Bullingdon Prison in support of Barrie Horne who had started a hunger strike to draw the attention of the public to the lies of the Labour Government and to demand that they kept their pre-election promise to hold a Royal Commission on vivisection.
3 Written by Hill Grove campaigner Sue Dickens.

"You'll no doubt be interested to know that thousands of pounds worth of damage has been done here today and cats stolen," he said, with a hint of a grin on his face. We had noticed the helicopter and police cars with sirens going in the opposite direction as we came down the main road. We talked to the officer who said that he loved cats and didn't approve of what went on at Hill Grove but he had to do his job.

We drank coffee and he shared biscuits with us. Suddenly a vision of hate and fury appeared from behind the gate, rushed up, pushed the officer aside, spat in the car window at me and then proceeded to hammer his fists on the car. Not wanting to risk damage to a friend's car, I backed up quickly. The fury then picked up a large rock which the officer wrestled away from him getting him behind the gate again.

After our hearts had settled, we noticed that the windscreen was cracked so I asked the officer to take action.

"He is a worker at Hill Grove, he's very angry because of today," he said.

"I am sure he is but that's got nothing to do with us, we've only just arrived so I want him arrested," I replied.

By now another police vehicle arrived and several officers plus a civilian were on their way to the farm. None of them would take any action and told us to leave.

I refused until I got their numbers and promised them that a formal complaint would be made against them. Back home I wrote a letter to the Chief Constable while the incident was fresh in my mind. A few days later I got a reply and the wheels were set in motion. In spite of the fact that we said we would be witnesses of the assault on the police officer, our assailant, Brian Butler was only charged with a Section 5 offence.

Christopher Brown dealt with any letters about the case. Their defence was that we had refused to leave a private driveway. Probably because the police officer's statement refuted this,

Butler pleaded guilty at the last minute. Consequently, we didn't get a chance to give our evidence in court and the magistrates did not award any damages, suggesting that the attack upon us had occurred during "an inflammatory situation." That was our first experience of Hill Grove justice.

Reporting the Magistrates Court hearing on October 18th, the *Oxford Mail* chose the most salient facts under the heading, 'Manager spat at protester.' The paper reported the prosecutor as saying Butler had begun "hitting the windscreen with his fist and spat through the window." Defence counsel Julian Smith said on behalf of his client, "He accepts he lost his temper and there was perhaps a misguided sense of loyalty to his employer."[3]

What would have happened to us if we had pushed a policeman aside, spat at a car driver, hammered on a car windscreen cracking it and then picked up a rock intent upon committing further damage? We took Butler to the small claims court determined that he would not get away with the attack. Because we had more witnesses than he did, the case was heard in Brighton. On two occasions Butler didn't turn up and in a letter sent to the court, Brown gave 'the harvest' as an excuse.

Eventually Brown sent a cheque to the court for £110, this was obviously cheaper than sending Butler to Brighton for the day. With the various expenses he should have paid £130, however, even after a letter from the court, he failed to pay the extra. The order still stands against him and can apparently affect his credit status.

Almost four months after the original Magistrates Court case and a year after the incident, the Crown Prosecution wrote to us, explaining why the magistrates had not granted us any compensation for the damage to our windscreen.[4]

---

3 *Oxford Mail*, October 18, 1997.
4 Principal Crown Prosecutor. January 5, 1998.

I am writing in reply to your faxed communications of the 15th October 1997. I am sorry that your letter was not replied to sooner.

The decision to prosecute Mr Butler for an offence contrary to Section 5 of the Public Order Act 1996 was made on the 22nd May 1997. It was considered that that charge was the most appropriate having regard to the available evidence. It was considered that that charge would encompass all of Mr Butler's conduct including the allegation that he spat at you and also the allegation that he struck your wind-screen.

Mr Butler entered a late plea of guilty to that offence on the 15th October 1997. He was fined £150 and was ordered to pay £40 towards the Prosecution costs. The prosecutor at court on the 16th October made an application for compensation on your behalf in respect of the damage caused to the windscreen of the car you were driving. The court would have been empowered to order compensation arising after the commission of an offence and it was the prosecution case that the striking of your windscreen was part and parcel of the Section 5 offence. No compensation was in fact ordered however because the court took the view that having regard to the statements of the prosecution witnesses it was not sufficiently clear that the damage sustained to the windscreen was a consequence of Mr Butler striking it.

"*Yes Minister*, we understand!" The Crown Prosecution Service had accepted the plea of guilty, so avoiding a trial, yet on the matter of the broken windscreen they had assessed the evidence in the privacy of their chambers, and without calling or hearing any witnesses found the defendant not guilty.

Sue Dickens

Chapter Eight

🐈 Cynthia Hands Over

"Well, well, we shall be strong enough. 'Thrice is he armed who hath his quarrel just'. We simply can't keep within the four corners of the law."[1]

When the battle really started, it was in with both feet at the deep end! The struggle to close Hill Grove farm changed radically in January 1997. The five years of hard continuous organising and pressure mounted by Cynthia and a hard core of persistent activists had, by 1997, attracted considerable attention. Following their example, large numbers of activists and ordinary people began to turn up at pickets and demonstrations.

Inevitably, as the battle intensified and the demonstrations grew, the other side began to fight back. In January activists managed to liberate 14 cats from Hill Grove farm, eight arrests were made and Christopher Brown went on the offensive in the *Oxford Mail*, for the first time.

They are completely misguided and misinformed. They have pretty evil minds and seem to think that people doing medical research have no respect for their animals. Vivisection is a bad word. The correct terminology is that they are for medical research. The whole purpose of breeding is to deliver virus free cats in a disease free unit. Cats are not used now as a laboratory animal except for veterinary research.[2]

---

1 Sherlock Holmes in *The Disappearance of Lady Carfax* by Sir Arthur Conan Doyle.
2 *The Oxford Mail* January 21, 1997.

ACT-AV campaigned and lobbied Parliamentary candidates for the forthcoming election. Then early in May, Laura and Cynthia went again to tell Mr Bellamy's neighbours, with the aid of the megaphone, about what was going on at the University. This time, however, a member of the Bellamy family struck back with an attack on Cynthia.

Son attacked activist's car

The son of a top Oxford University Administrator was released with a police caution after smashing an animal rights protestor's car window. Colin Bellamy, 26, of Wilmot Close, Witney, was arrested on Tuesday evening after Cynthia O'Neill's window was smashed. Mrs O'Neill was one of a small group of animal rights activists protesting outside Mr Bellamy's father's house in Witney. Godfrey Bellamy is Chief Administrator at Oxford University's department of physiology where vivisection is sometimes carried out. Mrs O'Neill said: "We had been there for three or four minutes with a loudspeaker when Mr Bellamy's son came out and karate kicked my window.[3]

Cynthia couldn't believe the dual standards operated by the police. She said later, "had I kicked in his windscreen I'd have been in a police cell for three days." While the demonstrators had been punished on a number of occasions for peacefully protesting, the other side was apparently able to mount a physical attack on a person with impunity. Giving a caution to Colin Bellamy enabled him to avoid paying the cost of the car window until Cynthia recouped the money by taking him to the small claims court. Cynthia, however, remained adamant that making Colin Bellamy pay for a broken car window was no compensation for the suffering and distress caused her by the attack. Bellamy had smashed the driver's side window with a kick, which only missed Cynthia's face by inches. She suffered trigeminal neuralgia and serious shock.

---

3 *The Witney Gazette*, April 23, 1997.

More and more protestors were joining the Sunday and weekday demos, especially with the summer sunshine. All new friends were given handbills listing letters to write to the Tourist Board, Advertising Authority, and West Oxfordshire District Council, The Caravan Club and *Your Cat* magazine. The pressure was mounting.

To signal people to one of the major Sunday demonstrations which the campaign had begun to organise, after appealing for boxes and string, Cynthia tied placards to convenient posts at the side of the Oxford roads at five and six o'clock in the morning. The early May morning was cold and without gloves her hands were frozen but she put up as many instructive placards as she could manage before the heavier traffic began.

When the protest began to grow and have a noticeable impact, one of the first weapons in the other side's armoury was the accusation that the demonstrators were costing the community money. Early in 1997, the first newspaper stories began to appear about the waste of taxpayers' money. By this time, over £20,000 of public money had been spent protecting one family and their business.

Demos a Waste of Police Time

Angry parish councillor, Sybil Williams, says she is disgusted by the amount of police time needed to keep the peace at Hill Grove farm, Minster Lovell, which breeds cats for medical research. "We can't afford to pay for an extra teacher at our village school and here they are running up a massive police bill," she said. "It is taxpayers' money and it's exorbitant." Miss Williams, 76, launched her attack on anti-vivisection campaigner Cynthia O'Neill, who is helping to organise weekly protests outside the farm. Miss Williams said "I am disgusted. This woman has a right to make a peaceful objection but there is a limit." Angry Miss Williams exchanged words with Mrs O'Neill when the campaigner disrupted a parish meeting last week, forcing the police to be called. Mrs O'Neill, who lives in Milton-Under-Wychwood, says "the protests will continue until the cat-breeding unit is closed down." [4]

---

4 *The Witney Gazette*, May 1997.

As the demonstrations grew in size so did the coverage and the argument in the local press. By now, there were more and more letters being published. In June, Cynthia and another campaigner demonstrated outside a garden party held for Imperial Cancer Research volunteers. Although the protest was completely peaceful the police were called.[5]

The Novice

Having read two letters in the Witney Gazette, I wrote to thank the writers for exposing the evil of vivisection. One of them, Cynthia, scenting another recruit, visited me almost immediately to discuss how I might help.

My first trip to Brown's home was a unique experience. Never before having used a megaphone, I was parked outside his house chanting "farmer Brown, we're going to close you down" watching the curtains twitching and inviting him to come out, when some policemen appeared before me. They might have been reading the Riot Act, but as I assured them, I couldn't hear because my hearing-aid battery had gone. I'm told Thames Valley police would have liked to arrest me, but they had a public image problem on their hands. A pity, at ninety three, my arrest might have got our message on the fraudulence and evil of vivisection in the national newspapers.

The campaign was a growing force getting on with the job intended. ACT-AV held strategy meetings and planned all night demos which had been so effective at Consort.[6]

---

5 *Oxford Mail,* June, 17th 1997.
6 Consort Kennels near Ross-on-Wye in Herefordshire bred beagles for vivisection. After a nine month campaign by the Consort Beagle Campaign, they closed down and 200 dogs were rehomed.

Some of the demonstrators were soon to be banned by a High Court injunction from going within a quarter of a mile of the cat farm. These High Court injunctions did of course get a lot of publicity but, to Brown's frustration, some protesters feeling that they were wrong ignored them completely. Due to the High Court Injunction, Cynthia measured out the quarter of a mile exactly and there she stood and sat. Her position was almost opposite the entrance to Dry Lane and with a nice loud megaphone the air adequately carried her messages. The injunctions didn't seem to do the job hoped of them.

New injunctions banning marches and demonstrations near Hill Grove farm did, however, lead to a change in tactics and the first march through Witney on July 13th 1997. There were clear, if only slight, signs that the campaign was having a serious effect. The police presence began to increase at each demonstration.

Following pressure from the campaign and constant letter writing, the Browns' caravan site was withdrawn from the Caravan Club listings in July 1997. Later that year, the campaign hit on a very effective propaganda tactic. Funds were collected to print a full colour 6 x 4 foot picture of Prof. Feldberg of London vivisecting a cat. The £200 poster, full of blood and guts, hit the other side hard. It was a recent picture and could not be denied. Police officers constantly asked that the poster be taken down but the campaigners' answers were always adamant. "No we won't. That's the idea of it. This is where the cats go. It's designed to make you think."

The campaigners learned that the Browns were highly thought of in their local church. Mr Brown held the title of Electoral Roll Leader. Members of the Parish Council, who originally passed his plans to enlarge the cattery, and Jack Straw, Home Office Minister, all worshiped St. Kenelm's, in Minster Lovell, Brown's church.

Cynthia was so furious that the Church accepted a parishioner who farmed cats for vivisection, that one Sunday in August she decided to protest at the church. Plucking up courage and at an opportune time in the Service, without, in her words being "rude or offensive", she asked for prayers for the Hill Grove campaign, prayers that the farm would cease its cruel trade and most vehemently of all, asked that the Browns be excommunicated!

In the summer of 1997, Cynthia O'Neill handed over the running of the growing campaign to Heather James and Greg Jennings, who had been involved in the successful campaign to force the closure of Consort Breeders.

With Heather and Greg's involvement, The Hill Grove Campaign became the campaign to Save The Hill Grove Cats. A newsletter was launched with a determination to increase the number of campaigners and step up the frequency of the demonstrations. The original core of the campaign engineered by Cynthia continued to have a life of its own. While the original campaigners had placed the emphasis on the fact that *vivisection is scientific fraud*, the new leadership focused on the cruelty to the cats which they considered was implicit in their factory farming and later abuse as objects of vivisection.

Cynthia was pleased to see a new strength being generated by the campaign, working so relentlessly she had become very tired. Heather and Greg brought a new focus and almost 'professional' organising abilities to the campaign. Cynthia, determined not to be redundant, still worked night and day, especially on fund-raising to cover the campaign's growing printing expenses.

Brilliant newsletters were produced and often Heather would bring me round my batch of 100 or so as late as half past eleven at night, always clutching her mobile phone saying "We'll get there, we're bound to." I've seen Heather with a black eye caused by police brutality and her friends have seen her lifted bodily by her hair by a policeman on horseback. "What keeps you going Heather? You look knackered," I would ask her. Her red bleary eyes from lack of sleep turn into a gentle smile as she says "It will close, it's bound to." I remember on one occasion Heather and Greg going to Scotland to give a talk. Rather than spend any campaign money, they slept in the car on their way up there and back. No plush hotels, no expensive four course meals and not even a comfortable bed for these two weary, hard working, and dedicated Hill Grove campaigners.

Chapter Nine

🐈 Poisoned!

The symptoms of acute poisoning (from Organo-Phosphorous com-pounds) appear to be adequately explained by the destruction of cho-linesterase and consequent toxic excess of acetylcholine: contraction of the pupils, headaches, photophobia; bronchial spasm; abdominal pain, nausea, vomiting, diarrhoea; muscular weakness, twitchings, convulsions, asphyxia, death.[1]

The night before the demonstration on the Sunday July 6th 1997, someone planned and carried out, what could have been a lethal counter-strike against the demonstrators. Demonstrators, protes-ters and police found that the area around the front of Hill Grove farm had been sprayed with a toxic substance, later proved to be organophosphate pesticide. 40 of the 200 protesters at the site, and an unknown number of police officers, fell ill, some seriously, after the exposure. Despite the fact that this was a serious crime against the person, no investigation was ever carried out and no one was arrested in relation to it. Matthew Kalman a freelance journalist wrote about the attack in *The Independent*:[2]

1 Dr Franklin Bicknell. *Chemicals in Food & in Farm Produce: their harmful effects.* Faber and Faber, London 1960.
2 *The Independent on Sunday*, September 21, 1997.

Animal activists fall ill after farm protest

Animal rights activists who fell ill after protesting outside a cat-breeding farm may have been poisoned by an organophosphate pesticide spray. Environmental health officers have found "substantial amounts" of a potentially lethal organophosphate pesticide called "dimethoate", on the roadside verge where protesters stand outside the Oxfordshire farm, which breeds cats for medical experiments. At a July demonstration outside Hill Grove farm, near Witney, activists initially noticed a chemical smell and yellowing of a 20yard stretch of grass, which serves as the centre for protest. Sixteen activists subsequently reported unexplained symptoms including nausea, sore throats, head pains and breathing difficulties. Exposure to organophosphate pesticides may be one of the causes of Gulf War Syndrome and one of the severe illnesses contracted by farmers after using certain sheep dips. The owner of Hill Grove farm, Chris Brown, dismissed suggestions that he had sprayed the verge. "I'm not concerned at all," he said "I don't know who did it." "The protesters did not need to be there and locals are getting fed up with them," he said, "I don't honestly think it was spilt by accident. I have got a suspicion but I'm not foolish enough to say who my suspicions are about. They'll do anything to discredit me. Dimethoate is an outdated pesticide and not one we use anyway."

Sheila English, a protestor who had eaten her lunch at the site, said: "The next day I had ulcers on my tongue. Three days later I got terrible pains in my throat and mouth and my air passages started to close up." Another protestor, who did not want to be named, said: "On the day after, I began to feel queasy and suffered with diarrhoea. I felt sick for over two weeks. I am usually a fit person and can shake off bugs easily."

Dr. Robert Davies, who has treated 60 sheep farmers for low-level organophosphate poisoning, said "dimethoate" could have caused the protesters' symptoms. "The symptoms described by the protesters are almost identical to those experienced by sheep farmers when they dip. Dipper's flu consists of symptoms including muscular aches and pains, general lassitude and lethargy, feeling awful, in some cases tightness of the chest, and mild depression."

The use of organophosphates against people harks back to military use. They were developed by the Nazis in the late 1930s as nerve agents and are precursors to the sarin nerve gas used in the 1995 Tokyo subway attack. "It's very worrying if derivatives of military nerve agents are now being used as, how shall I say, weapons, if that indeed is the case," said Dr. Davies. There was no agricultural reason for spraying the pesticide on the verge, he added.

West Oxfordshire's principal Environmental Health Officer, Keith Walton, who collected samples for analysis after the incident, confirmed the "dimethoate" found was dangerous. "The analyst's opinion was that the levels were such that there may be possible health implications," he said. The council does not spray organophosphates. Police involved in supervising the protests are also concerned they may have been contaminated.

"From our enquiries we have no evidence of who put it there," said Superintendent Pauline Sydenham of Thames Valley Police. "It could have been the protesters for all we know. It certainly wasn't us. We're concerned about our officers in addition to those other people who were present", she said.

Christine Gosden, Professor of Medical Genetics at Liverpool University, has written to Jack Straw, the Home Secretary, whose weekend cottage is less than a mile from the farm, to press him to look into the health effects on police and protesters.

Cynthia wrote to the *Independent on Sunday*[3] criticising the assumption of Superintendent Pauline Sydenham of Thames Valley Police that the protesters might have poisoned themselves. This mad idea, the chemical equivalent of "He threw himself down the steps to the cell, your honour", echoes the view voiced by Christopher Brown. Cynthia's letter ended: "A most serious crime has been committed. The criminal should be found without delay, or what next?" Indeed this was a serious question. Someone had tried to harm the protesters using a toxic nerve agent. The only people who could act decisively were the police. But the police, despite illnesses suffered by their own officers, seemed to be opposed to finding a culprit.

---

3 *The Independent on Sunday*, September 28,1997.

Cynthia later reported the following conversation with police officers after she had first sensed that something was wrong. "Excuse me, there's a horrible smell, the grass is yellow/brown and there is weed killer or something put down. Please can you contact the council for us." The reply was facetious: "There is a chemical factory nearby. We haven't got the phone number for the council."

Cynthia eventually pushed the West Oxfordshire District Council Environmental Health Department into testing the soil; even then, they insisted that the campaign must pay for the tests.

Following our recent series of telephone conversations I can confirm that substantial amounts of organophosphates pesticide dimethoate were found in the pooled samples of the verge I sent for analysis. The analyst's opinion was that the levels were such that there may be possible health implications. As I said previously other tests were negative so a mass spectrometer analysis was done.

Dimethoate is a broad spectrum contact and systemic insecticide used on a variety of crops. For your information I have contacted the Health and Safety Executive Agricultural Division, the Environment Agency and the Oxfordshire County Council who may have an interest in the outcome of the analysis from possible enforcement point of view.

I should point out that just because this chemical was found in the sample it does not say or indicate or intimate or imply who put it there, it says simply that the chemical was found.[4]

A poisoned protestor

I am a mother, grandmother and housewife. I have held the position of Carer in a residential home for the elderly. When my children were younger I was a playgroup helper and a committee member for the Mother and Toddler group, also the PTA committee. In more recent years I co-founded the Ashford Greenpeace Support Group.

---

4 K.R. Dalton, Principal Environmental Health Officer. August 20, 1997.

I am against research involving animals or any animal-linked experiments. I believe that money used for animal research and vivisection would be better used to seek alternative methods of research. I believe I am entitled to protest peacefully against vivisection, as I believe it is unnecessary and morally wrong. I believe that the more people I can give information to about vivisection the higher the number of people protesting against vivisection will be. I am a peaceful citizen and other than two cases of obstruction, I have no convictions against me.

I am normally in good health. It is many years since I had flu. I never get coughs or colds and my menstruation is very regular. On the 6th July 1997 I arrived at Hill Grove farm, Minster Lovell, at approximately midday. I sat on both sides of the road on the grass verge, in three different places, for a total of about one and a half hours. The remainder of the time I spent on footpaths around the farm, later moving back to outside the drive. Here I smelt a smell that I was not familiar with.

We returned to the minibus but had mechanical problems. Later we walked back down the lane to Hill Grove farm whilst we were waiting for a mechanic. We walked around and back to the minibus. Several of us commented on the strange smell outside Hill Grove farm. We waited and it was after 11.00pm before we left.

Once on the minibus it was soon obvious I was not at all well. I put it down to tiredness through waiting. My throat was dry and my voice was hoarse, I had a peculiar discomfort like an itch deep inside my chest. I had a feeling like a tight band around my head.

By the time I reached home and for the next few days I had pains in my head and hardly any voice at all. It was two weeks before my voice was restored. During Monday 7th July I began to cough. It was a dry cough. I felt that if I didn't cough I would choke. It was not a cough coming from the throat but a peculiar cough that seemed to rise from low in the chest, giving me a choking feeling.

By Thursday 10th July the cough was at its worst. From Friday onwards it became less frequent. Just as I thought it had gone, I would cough again. I am still troubled with it at night and early morning. It is now 13 weeks since the onset of the problem. On Wednesday 9th July I woke with a swelling in my mouth. It was on the lower lip, it was bluish in colour. During the next day the lump burst open and gave way to a large crack in my lip, this took over two weeks to heal. Healing was hampered by the need to cough. I kept getting pains in my head. During the following weeks, I had three bouts of flu-type symptoms. I had pains deep in the muscles of my limbs, sweating and a deep dull headache. On the weekend of the 23/24th August the cough became more frequent again.

My menstrual period was very late. Due on the 10th July, it finally came on the 29th August. This was followed by another menstrual period on the 12th September. This was totally abnormal for me, as my periods have always been regular.

My husband was getting very concerned about my health. He was especially worried as I am usually so fit. I was also getting worried so I decided to see a doctor. My GP sent me for a chest x-ray and said she would speak to the poisons unit at Guy's Hospital for advice. The x-ray did not show any foreign bodies in the lungs. An exhaling test showed decreased movement.

My GP was able to observe that the exertion of this simple test brought on a bout of coughing. She said the cough obviously indicated I had ingested a substance which was irritating the lining of my lungs. To ease the irritation she suggested an asthma type steroid inhaler. I declined the inhaler, as my GP was unable to tell me as to whether it had been tested on animals. As I said earlier, I am opposed to animal testing. I explained about my menstrual cycle, as I am concerned about this. My GP said that something had obviously interfered with the normal functioning of my body but now it seemed to be correcting itself.

I recently visited my local police station, as I believe someone had poisoned me. They were very unhelpful and said it was a civil matter and not a police matter. I wrote to the Chief of Kent police about my visit to Hill Grove farm, my health problems since then, the soil sample and the lack of interest at Ashford police station.

I have received a reply, which states my letter has been forwarded to the Chief Constable of Thames Valley Police, for whatever action he deemed necessary. I believe that someone sprayed or poured organophosphate pesticide or insecticide on the public areas outside Hill Grove farm, Minster Lovell, prior to my visit there on the 6th July. Whoever did this would be aware that people would be sitting and standing and eating food there. I am now very worried and concerned about my future health as I have read that exposure to organophosphates can lead to cancers, cardiovascular problems and damage to the central nervous system.

My husband is prepared to testify as to my health problems. He is very worried. Two friends who I have met weekly for the last two and a half years are both prepared to give evidence as to my previous health and how it has deteriorated since the 6th July. They were shocked at the severity of my cough and the boil on my lip. They also know that my menstrual periods were regular.

I have made this statement for use by the police or as part of a private prosecution.

———◇❖◇———

Cynthia worked hard to get someone to take responsibility for the serious crime which had been committed but the authorities seemed incapable of understanding campaigners as citizens vulnerable to crime. Cynthia's GP was so upset about her illness brought on by the pesticide that he wrote to the police complaining on her behalf. Cynthia sought advice about medical measures which might be taken to alleviate the symptoms of OP exposure and sent out instructions to all known affected protesters, suggesting courses of vitamin C, beta-carotene and vitamin A in large doses. This therapy would cost each person around £22. For a long time after the incident many protesters linked cardiac problems, which occurred amongst them, with the OP exposure.

Chapter Ten

🐈 The First Coach Arrives

These pathetic dropouts are people with nothing better to do except organising mayhem and anarchy at their will.[1]

Protesters were by now descending upon Witney and Hill Grove farm in increasing numbers. The very first coach from Brighton arrived on a hot summer evening during a vigil at the Martyr's Memorial. Some time before, Kate had vouched for the coach, "you wait and see. We're a hard working lot down at Brighton. I promise. I won't let you down."

More protesters were joining in the night vigils which also kept the police and the force helicopter occupied. To take the campaign into the public arena, Heather and Greg arranged a public meeting at the Corn Exchange in Witney. Thames Valley Police showed their true colours during the meeting, making it clear that they were more interested in criminalizing the activists than supporting free speech. Uniformed police were at the door of the Corn Exchange making the meeting appear somehow dangerous and police camera operators were spotted in an open window of a hotel opposite the venue. The hotel would have helped the police –they hosted the weekly lunch for the Rotary Club of which farmer Brown was a member.

---

1 Angry Witney resident. *Witney Gazette.*

The Browns, naming Cynthia and Natasha, took out a High Court injunction now ordering the duo half a mile away from the farm. To avoid the effect of the High Court injunction banning marches near Hill Grove, an August march complete with whistles, banners and a megaphone took place from the farm to Witney town centre. By now, however, there was saturation policing. On the march into Witney town centre, the police outnumbered demonstrators. Police on horseback and a helicopter were present at every demonstration.

After the campaign found that Jack Straw, New Labour's Home Secretary, had a home in the Cotswolds they targeted it for vigils and pickets, so stretching police resources even further.

After an attack on the premises of Witney Farm Supplies, who were providing Hill Grove farm with goods, Mr Brown was asked to take his custom elsewhere. All night vigils proved effective and several protesters visited the homes of the cat farm workers. Police, overstretched by the number of campaign targets, began arresting protesters at random for prefabricated offences such as "using a loud hailer."

In October 1997, the free *Oxford Journal* led with a front page story headlined Horror of Cat Trade.[2] The newspaper always reported campaign events with accuracy and excellent photographs. As a result of the article and complaints made by protesters, New Labour MP for Birmingham, Selly Oak, Dr. Lynne Jones, asked the Home Office to allow the RSPCA to visit the farm. Suzanne Hubbard in the *Oxford Mail*[3] wondered when the last inspection by the Home Office took place at the farm and whether any irregularities were discovered. She too suggested that the RSPCA should inspect the premises. An RSPCA spokeswoman, Julie Briggs, said Inspectors had attempted to visit Hill Grove two years previously but were refused access.

---

2 *Oxford Journal*, October 3, 1997.
3 *Oxford Mail*, October 16, 1997.

Anyone who had observed the campaign over the last few years would realise that some people who might have previously been opposed to the objectives of the protesters were now beginning to prepare bolt holes to safe political ground, in the event of a campaign victory.

In October 1997, protesters attending a night vigil were again exposed to pesticides. Eight campaigners became ill. In another demonstration, three women were assaulted by police dogs and one woman was bitten on her arm.[4]

Not a week went by without something in the newspapers about vivisection. A big protest on Sunday 16th November produced photographs and coverage in the *Daily Telegraph*, *The Times*, the *Daily Express* and *Police Review*. The campaign was now making national news and it was not unusual to see the whole of the front page of the local newspaper given over to the growing campaign.

The *Oxford Courier* obtained an exclusive interview with an ex-farm worker.

Horror of Hill Grove farm by a girl who worked there

The woman we spoke to who used to work at Hill Grove farm said she was so upset by conditions at the farm she had to leave. The 24-year-old ex-farm worker, who has chosen to remain anonymous, was responsible for scrubbing the cat pens out, feeding the animals and changing their litter trays. But she said she was shocked to discover what conditions at the farm were really like. She said: "Chris Brown is not an animal lover at all. They were just numbers to him."

She lasted two months at the farm before telling him she thought his business was "cruel and disgusting." She said: "I was disgusted when I found out he tattooed the cat's ears. He claimed it didn't hurt them but they used to squeal with pain. It was awful."

---

4 Sylvia O'Brien was later awarded compensation for damages.

But Mr Brown insists that he must tattoo the animals in accordance with Home Office regulations. "The Home Office told us that all primates, cats and dogs bred for scientific purposes should be 'clearly and adequately identifiable by an acceptable method of marking agreed with Inspectors' in the establishment in which they are bred. This can involve tattooing but other methods can be used." The ex-worker also said: "A lot of cats were born deformed and their mothers would eat them. I found several cats dead for no apparent reason."

Mr Brown admitted some cats were born deformed and their mothers ate them but said that this was a natural occurrence in the wild. He said: "This is why you don't find many deformed cats around." The ex-Hill Grove worker added that the cats were nervous of Mr Brown. She said: "They used to go mad when he came in, climbing the walls of their cages." Cats were frequently ill and suffered from diarrhoea a lot. We used to report such illnesses to Mr Brown and the next day the cats that were ill just disappeared." Mr Brown laughed at these suggestions and said that this was "a complete lie."

The ex-employee at the farm said she was also horrified to discover the cramped spaces the cats had to live in. She said: "Because of the confined space, a lot of them used to fight. Many were kittens. They had no bedding and no toys to play with."

Mr Brown also refuted these suggestions saying: "The cats have sawdust for bedding and climbing frames to play with." He added that there were only between one and twenty cats in each pen, but he was not prepared to discuss how much space they had to live in. The ex-farm worker added: "Farmer Brown claims that there is a vet at the farm quite often, but I never saw a vet and I never saw any Inspectors."

She said that cats were only fed once a day and said that 40 cats frequently had to share just 12 tins of cat food. Mr Brown also denied this, saying: "Why would I want to starve my cats?" He also insisted our source could be someone who broke into his farm earlier this year. But the ex-Hill Grove worker added: "I think the protesters should carry on demonstrating. He will close down eventually."

Save the Hill Grove Cats are holding a 24-hour vigil at the farm this weekend.

The Campaign was later to find out that over the years several of the cattery staff, becoming aware of the cats' fate, did smuggle some out to safety. They also got to know of good vets in the area who had asked no questions.

With night and day demonstrations increasing, more activists ended up in court. Farmer Brown too had to give evidence in many hearings and the campaigners sensed that he was now finding it all a bit much. It was not unusual for fifteen protesters on a night vigil to have a hundred police in attendance!

On the 22nd November 1997, Rev. James Thompson conducted another open air service, this time beside the A40 opposite to Dry Lane.

The campaign's most successful year so far ended with a hundred police officers surrounding the cat farm as five carol singers blended their voices of protest with the chill December air.

Chapter Eleven

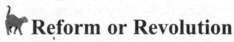 **Reform or Revolution**

Like human beings, the mother-newborn bond is strong within our feline friends. I wonder how farmer Brown would like to have a new-born daughter or son removed for vivisection.[1]

Many protesters and members of the public wrote to the RSPCA seeking advice and guidance on the Hill Grove issue. The RSPCA brought out their own leaflet on Hill Grove farm called *Your Questions Answered*. This leaflet was reprinted in the Hill Grove Campaign newsletter[2], to inform the campaigners of the position of the RSPCA.

RSPCA HILL GROVE FARM
-YOUR QUESTIONS ANSWERED-

There has recently been a series of demonstrations at Hill Grove farm trying to close the establishment down. Hill Grove is licensed by the Government to breed and supply cats for research. None of us want cats to be used in this way, and closing Hill Grove down may seem a simple solution to the problem. However, in fact this is unlikely to make any difference to the use of cats in UK laboratories, and may even add significantly to the animals' suffering. This fact sheet explains why, and why we need to look for other

---

1 Pete Merson-Davies a Hill Grove Prisoner.
2 Issue no. 3, Jan/Feb 1998.

more effective and permanent solutions to help the animals. It describes the RSPCA's approach, and what you can do to help.

WHAT IS HILL GROVE FARM?

Hill Grove farm breeds and supplies cats for use in research. It is licensed by the Home Office under the 1986 UK Animals (Scientific Procedures) Act (ASPA) and it has to comply with the Home Office Code of Practice for the housing and care of animals. This sets the standards for the husbandry and care of animals, including the minimum size of pen that the cats can be housed in, and when the kittens can be weaned and sold. The research establishments that buy Hill Grove cats are also licensed by the Home Office under ASPA, as is each individual programme of research, and each person carrying it out. The law requires that the perceived benefits of the research be weighed against the effects on the animals before a licence is granted and that for cats, dogs and primates, a special case must be made for using them.

ARE PET CATS USED IN RESEARCH?

The law states that all cats used for research in the UK must be bred at the establishments where they are used or bought from breeders such as Hill Grove. Nevertheless, many people still worry that stolen or stray pets may be used. This does not mean that they do not care about the animals specifically bred for research, but they do not like to think of their own much loved companion in this situation. However, anyone who broke the law by using stray animals for research would soon be found out by a Home Office Inspector and be prosecuted, losing his or her licence to breed or work with animals. Researchers also need to know how old an animal is, where it came from and whether it has been exposed to any diseases; this would not be possible with a stolen or stray pet. The RSPCA has no evidence that stray or stolen animals are used and believes that it is highly unlikely that this occurs.

HOW MANY CATS ARE USED IN RESEARCH?

Information about the numbers of animals used in research, together with a limited amount of information on what they were used for, is published each year by the Home Office. Analysis of these figures by the RSPCA shows that around 1,500 cats are used each year in the UK. This accounts for 0.06% of the 2.6 million laboratory animals used every year in the country (over 80% are rats and mice). Most cats are used for biological research and human or veterinary medical studies. Some cats are used for pharmaceutical safety and efficacy testing. None are used to safety test cosmetics ingredients, household products or food additives.

WOULD CLOSING HILL GROVE END THE USE OF CATS IN RESEARCH?

Unfortunately the answer is no. The establishments that buy cats from Hill Grove would either add to their own animal breeding facilities or buy cats in from the continent or even the USA. If cats are imported from abroad, this will mean that in addition to the procedures they undergo when they reach a research establishment, they will also suffer the stress of a long journey. Thus, closing independent breeders down will not result in any significant reduction in animal use and could actually create even worse problems for individual animals.

In response to this RSPCA leaflet the Hill Grove Campaign issued the following statement.

WE URGE YOU TO WRITE NOW AND CONDEMN THE ACTIONS OF THE RSPCA.

We have just received a copy of a leaflet put out by the RSPCA called *Hill Grove farm – your questions answered*. It only mentions the campaign once, but it is a very cleverly worded attack on the Hill Grove campaign.

The leaflet starts off with *What is Hill Grove farm?* It describes Hill Grove in terms of the 1986 Animal Scientific

Procedures Act, Home Office code for the housing and care of animals. It does not say that Hill Grove does comply, only that it should.

The Animal Scientific Procedures Act covers the licence of premises by the Home Office and the RSPCA suggests that this Act protects and oversees the welfare of animals in places licensed i.e. Hill Grove farm.

In 1996 two long-standing workers at Huntingdon Life Sciences[3] (also licensed under the ASPA) were prosecuted for cruelty following an expose on *Channel 4*. This clearly shows the total inadequacy of the Act to protect animals.

It says, "The RSPCA has no evidence that stray or stolen animals are used and believes that it is highly unlikely that this occurs." They do say that they rarely go into laboratories, so how do they know that stolen animals are not used?

The RSPCA suggest that only 0.06% of the animals used in laboratories are cats, and that 80% are rats and mice. With 1,000 cats at Hill Grove farm at any one time, surely the issue is not how many cats are being used in Britain, but the fact that ALL the cats are destined for vivisection laboratories here or abroad? The RSPCA suggests that closing Hill Grove would result in extra stress for cats imported from abroad. What about the stress suffered by the thousands exported abroad each year from Hill Grove?

Unlike the RSPCA we believe it is morally wrong to use any animals in laboratories. Using over 2 million rats and mice a year in experiments is not something to cheer about!

They also say that if Hill Grove closes, laboratories will have to buy cats from other breeders in countries like the USA and they would add the stress of travelling to the stress involved in a lab. Some points they conveniently forget.

---

3 Huntingdon Life Sciences (HLS), an animal testing laboratory in Cambridge, has been the subject of four undercover investigations, revealing gross staff incompetence, falsification of data and animal cruelty. The company is supported by the New Labour Government, which is heavily committed to vivisection and animal testing.

The cats at Hill Grove received little or no human comfort. That is OK in the wild but not stuck in a cage all its short life. When the RSPCA were asked to help the Consort dogs they declined and gave no help at all. With the £1.1 million in the bank they could have bought the dogs and never noticed.

Write to them now, the actions of the RSPCA are divisive and only serve to reduce the effectiveness of a genuine campaign aimed at protecting cats destined for vivisection labs.

A massive demonstration was planned for Lab Animals Day on the 18ᵗʰ April 1998. Cynthia was interviewed for a *BBC 2* film screened in January 1998. Although the film asked questions about the role of the police and was disparaging about the farm generally, many campaigners thought that it was clearly uncritical of vivisection. Much of what Cynthia said about vivisection was edited out of the film. *The Radio Times*[4] chose a colour picture of the Chief Constable of Thames Valley Police to advertise the programme. In the *BBC* film, Supt. Davies, who had been in charge of the police operation, admitted that on occasions when inside the premises, the police were effectively acting as Mr Brown's own private security force.[5]

From the land of song

We came with a song from Wales. Some Song! I laugh every time I sing those songs to myself. As I've often said, protest days were not all gloom.

From Pembrokeshire to Newport we filled our coach and sang our Hill Grove songs over the Severn Bridge through Swindon to Witney. We left with our own sand-

---

4 *The Radio Times,* January 17/ 23, 1998.
5 *Witney Gazette,* January 28, 1998.

wiches, drinks, placards and flags and varied our destination depending on last instructions from "base", we never knew quite what the "boys in blue" had in store for us.

Our first visit on 18th April 1998 was by car and we parked in a lay-by a bit up from Dry Lane, Minster Lovell. Dressed mostly in black we made our way down Dry Lane to the farm and passed the main entrance and proceeded to the stile, manned by the Thames Valley Police who examined our identities to weed out anyone with "form".

The path took us to a wood and a steep slope, which was a quagmire, and caused us to slither, slide and squelch to the bottom. We then crossed a field and followed the path up a wooded slope to the back of the farm. Here we found a heavy police presence mostly in riot gear.

A large wire fence, which had been forced to the ground on the previous visit, separated us from the farm and this fence. We carried on around the fence to an open field. Here the barricade looked like the exterior of a prison camp with police in watchtowers keeping an eye on our activities. Behind them were the sheds, the sheds we suspected housed the poor imprisoned cat victims, waiting their turn to be transported to laboratories all over the U.K. and as far away as Australia.

It was a sickening feeling seeing those sheds and feeling helpless. I was rather worried about the noise we were all making and wondering if it was frightening those poor cats and kittens. I expect so, but feeling ran high and what other action could we take? Missiles were hurled at the police and lobbed over the fence and from time to time the barricade parted and out charged the mounted brigade waving truncheons and meaning business.[6] Having ridden into the crowd and dispersed it, they then returned to the enclosure and the missiles flew again.

---

6 It was suggested in a later court case that police acting as agents provocateur had been responsible for throwing missiles.

Some of the younger and more impassioned protesters worked at demolishing the barricade but more charges and dispersals sent us off into the ploughed field at the front of the house. This field was full of stones and very soon a "chain" formed and the ammunition was fed to the "throwers" who aimed at the windows, roof tiles and electric wires.

Oddly enough the mounted police sat on their horses in a line for some time, just watching and doing nothing to stop the throwing. I felt that they were nearly condoning the action, but on reflection decided that they were probably videoing or noting the ringleaders. Suddenly they charged, scattering us in all directions. We then made our way back to the watchtowers and most resumed demolishing the barricades. A group of police was watching from the corner of the field and was getting nearer. Suddenly an enormous roar and cheer went up as a section of the barricade gave way. The mounted troops thundered out and charged into the middle of the "workers" and their close supporters and this is where I and my other old lady friend decided it was time to retreat, before we were charged at speed. We picked our way through to the quagmire area and clambered up the slippery slope making our way back to the car. We read about our escapade the next day.

Sunday 6th September 1998 was our next visit, which went to the Leys recreation ground. A rally with speakers, well attended and then a march through Witney towards Dry Lane, but only so far and then back again. Mobile phones gave us our final directions for many meetings and they varied depending on police plans. I missed the 'Christmas shopping in Oxford' demo of 12th December 1998 but heard it was a great success. After they lifted the "exclusion zone" at Hill Grove we were able to go down Dry Lane again, but not to the stile or anywhere near the house or buildings.

We had to do the best we could to let the Browns know we were thinking of them and made all the racket we could. This was our demo destination for some time, but we weren't really getting noticed enough by the public, being neatly tucked down the lane encased by police fences and mounted police keeping us from getting to the A40. The fence collapsed and over, somehow or other, we all went and headed for Witney and some managed to get round the back of the farm again. On the next visit we were even more organised by the police. Trapped in Dry Lane for a couple of hours, then 'frog marched' into Witney, turned round and 'frog marched' back to our coaches and transport. The police horses came perilously close to trampling us on many occasions and in fact did trample a mother and child crossing the field, with the mother ending up in hospital.

On another occasion, the 20th February 1999, we had promised our coach driver to be back at a specified time, so we decided to march part of the way to Witney and then beetle back to the coach. But the police had other ideas and said, "You wanted to march - so march!" One woman was pushed from behind and so was I, quite roughly. The other woman was an asthmatic and had an attack. She was allowed to sit on the pavement to recover. I loitered and seized my chance to get back to the coach to let our driver know what had happened. The others had to go all the way into Witney until finding the officer in charge, who allowed them to leave the march and race back to the coach exhausted.

Visiting Oxford on the 12th June 1999 amongst the tourists gave us good coverage and lots of leaflets were given out, so more and more people learnt what was going on on their doorstep and they were horrified. Some would argue that medical research was vital for progress in curing cancer and other diseases and using an animal was preferable to losing a human. I wonder about that!

A protester from Wales

Part Three

The Struggle Intensifies

105

Chapter Twelve

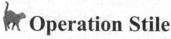 **Operation Stile**

> *The new legislation poses a tangible threat to civil liberties. While stalking another person can never be justified, harassment is sometimes deemed legitimate: as when a journalist harasses a corrupt politician... or union pickets harass strike-breakers when they go to work, or when peace protesters harass arms profiteers... This may sound perverse but is not a right to harass an important element in a free society.[1]*

At the end of January 1998, the police officially announced the setting up of a new task force to police the growing number of large demonstrations around Hill Grove farm. The police bill for monitoring the demonstrations then stood at £400,000. At the same time the campaign announced the setting up of a permanent camp outside the farm.

Operation Stile was based at Newbury Police Station and designed to bring the campaign and demonstrations to an end. The police strategy was nothing more sophisticated than mounting force and continuing harassment. Operation Stile was, however, more of a 'counter insurgency' operation than the previous ad hoc programme. It began by targeting known activists. Cynthia, Natasha and Lynn were all targeted.

Officers in Operation Stile responded furiously to a new campsite set up in the cold January of 1998. Despite the fact that the first tent was pitched on public ground, it was demolished and the tent poles broken in one police swoop.

---

1 Robert Fine. *Being Stalked: A Memoir.* Chatto & Windus, London 1997.

There were a number of camps set up outside the farm. Before the injunction prohibited Cynthia from driving past, she would broadcast news over a megaphone for campers. The first camp continued for a good few weeks until the weather became too cold. Money was collected for warm sleeping bags. Lynn, a hardened camper, confirmed that "It was cold. There was a frost and often ice in the water bucket."

Regular visitors climbed over the often-muddy footpath with water, candles, food and other items needed for basic survival. Cynthia was most impressed that Lynn had chosen to spend her valuable nights away from her job as a midwife. Camps came and went. A big campsite was finally planned but the police arrived en masse on the day threatening to arrest any drivers of parked vehicles.

Operation Stile picked off the "ring leader" of the campaign after the last camp had been broken up. Cynthia was arrested first using the megaphone outside the farm. "Stop working at Hill Grove farm, you know exactly what you are doing. The experiments on cats are nonsense when applied to human patients." Suddenly her time was up. Introducing a rare note of levity and surrealism into the proceedings, as she was lifted, Cynthia said, for reporting in any future court case: "Me speak no English. Me Chinese."

Cynthia was marched on her walking frame up the road by two police officers and charged under Section 11 of the Protection from Harassment Act. She was bundled with difficulty into a police van, taken to Witney police station where she was locked up, finger printed, photographed and detained for a few hours. Cynthia was the first of the Hill Grove protesters to be charged under the new Harassment Act, originally brought in to protect women against stalkers. Cynthia's bail conditions kept her a mile from the farm and excluded her from certain public roads in the area. Cynthia already had an injunction against her that with her fellow campaigners, she was now ignoring. One of the heavy costs of her arrested was the seizure of the ACT-AV megaphone.

Operation Stile also stepped up the psychological harassment of the main activists. Cris, a qualified lab technician, now turned antivivisectionist, was frequently told that he was a target for surveillance and at every demonstration he expected to be picked out. Lynn was also arrested but not charged and she later wrote to the *Oxford Mail*[2] outlining what she saw as a police strategy.

> As the police go into Judge Dredd mode at Hill Grove farm by smashing up our property, putting us under 24 hour surveillance, arresting us for the slightest little thing, making us take down our banners, beating us up and generally intimidating us, I would like to point out the more they behave in this way the more determined animal rights people will be to close down the cattery. At the moment we are even threatened with the Harassment Act which was never intended to curb peaceful protest. By doing this, the cost to the taxpayer will surely escalate. The whole operation will only protect the interests of the vivisection industry, as no one that I know has any intention of harming farmer Brown or his workers. How sad that his profits are given priority over other public concerns. It is time to ask questions as to why this should be the case. One thing should be made abundantly clear, we are not afraid of the police or local vigilantes. Our consciences remain clear and we have no intention of going away. I would, however, like to compliment some police officers on their fair and good-humoured approach towards us.

In the local press, the clamour grew over the considerable cost of the policing. Increasingly, caught between wanting the campaign to end while not wanting to give Christopher Brown succour, more and more pundits were asking for the police to be withdrawn and Brown left to fend for himself. Local Councillors, pressured by local residents, were forced to discuss ways to close the cat farm. The *Witney Gazette* reported Mr Ted Cooper, the Labour councillor for Witney South, as saying: "Some way has got to be found to stop this evil practice?"[3]

---

2 *Oxford Mail*, February 11, 1998.
3 *Witney Gazette*, February 18, 1998.

Through the grapevine, the campaign had learned that the Home Office had given orders to Thames Valley Police to keep Hill Grove open at all costs, even using water cannons and CS gas. CS gas had been used against unprotected animal activists at Consort Breeding Kennels.

A February Demonstration

February's demonstration in 1998 drew a thousand campaigners and the police made twenty arrests during what the *Gazette* glibly referred to as "flaring violence." The *Gazette* reported the police deployment by Thames Valley Police as "280 officers, including 30 from Gloucestershire. The force helicopter watched from the air and officers on horseback patrolled the perimeters of the farm."[4]

Cynthia was unable to join in and forced to keep watch on her one-mile boundary line. It was tough, but she managed to wave-in many coaches, vans and carloads. Bathed in brilliant sunshine, this chill February morning had a special air of expectancy about it.

Most of the national newspapers covered the demonstration. Sue Parslow, editor of *Your Cat*, had been receiving letters and requests for news coverage of the campaign for some years and finally a long article in colour appeared in the March 1998 edition of the magazine. This article alerted thousands more to the farm.

One Saturday night in March there was another successful liberation; 13 cats were quietly freed. How had the police who ringed the farm failed to apprehend the young balaclava-clad activists racing over the fields?

Lynn joined Cynthia and others in the exclusive one-mile club. Gradually, on protest days, the excluded campaigners began to have their own demonstrations at a distance.

---

4 *Witney Gazette,* February 25, 1998.

Hundreds of new people came forward in the first months of 1998, as if in answer to the new strategy of Operation Style. The campaigners realised that the momentum of a mass movement had its own strength. One part of the battle moved from the surrounds of the farm to the Magistrate's Court in Witney, which witnessed a regular stream of defendants and police.

Cynthia thought it an important part of the campaign for activists to be in court giving support to defendants. As often as possible, she attended the court despite the fact that she found it emotionally distressing seeing innocent, compassionate, kind and brave people roughly bundled off in prison vans.

Despite the fact that courts are public places, the police frequently tried to stop campaigners observing court cases. Police videos of demonstrations always worked in favour of the police, who, being in charge of this evidence, cut and edited the film to support their story. Cynthia was sure that the reason the police tried to stop her from attending court was that they did not want observers to see the edited video films they had prepared. Everything was done to convince the magistrates that the protester before them were 'terrorists'. To counter the police videos more campaigners acquired camcorders. It was clear, however, that the police did not like being filmed and often these camcorders were smashed.

An Arrest at Hill Grove Farm

I had been involved in a few demonstrations over recent times before I first went to Hill Grove. I tried to maintain an unprejudiced view of the police on my first visits, despite my experiences on foxhunts. It was soon clear to me that they were treating us slightly differently; there was a definite coldness and suspicion in the air around many of the cops, while others were openly hostile and aggressive.

At the first demo I bumped into Steve. Steve and I worked together a few years previously. He was now working for an anti-vivisection group 'Uncaged', who had raised money to buy a few of the beagles from Consort. Consort had bred dogs for experiments before they were closed down by an intense campaign against them. The liquidators were selling all stock, including the dogs. After talking to Steve, we agreed to take one, and spent the next few months rehabilitating Eddy. Watching with joy and despair as he discovered new freedoms, showed us his mental scars and destroyed what we owned. Eddy came with us to Hill Grove on many occasions, and was known far better than I was among the regular demonstrators.

The experience of being among so many new friends was invaluable to Eddy's development and I still feel bringing him did him the world of good. On February 22nd 1998 we travelled to the farm for a demonstration. My wife, Tracy, sat in front while Eddy sat in the back with Oak, a friend from a local group. Eddy threw up in the back seat. I cleared it up and shoved it in a plastic bag in my pocket. Later, I overcame the temptation to leave the copper who searched me to discover it the hard way, warning the poor guy first.

We demonstrated at the farm, then went off on a march to Witney. The police were looking frustrated at the way things were going. Not only were we calling the shots, none of us were acting in a violent or destructive way. There was a good-natured determination among the crowd who defied all attempts to categorise them according to age or social background.

As we assembled in the High Street, a retired priest spoke of the way in which he felt actions like ours mirrored those of Jesus Christ. After the speeches, we went back along the main road to the farm. On the road outside the farm there were a few incidents which I did'nt see. I missed the arrest of Soraya Marchani, but saw the shaking heads and words of disgust from the many who had seen the slight girl dragged, wrenched and bundled into a police van by police who were beginning to forget that they should at least make some attempt to hide frayed tempers.

I found myself at one point peering ahead to a point where voices were raised, but again I couldn't see what was happening. I looked back and realised that I was on my own in the middle of the road, the rest of the demonstrators held back by a police line. It would be better to be with them, and it crossed my mind to try to get back, but as it would involve approaching the police from behind, the prospects of an elbow in the face became obvious. I stayed put.

Seconds later a copper approached. "Come on, back with the other lot," he said, trying to sound authoritative. I felt there was provocation in everything they were doing now, so I smiled and nodded. "Yes I will go, no need to…!" But before I knew it he was moving in on me and another joined in. I was on the floor almost immediately and curled up with my hands over my head like a foetus. They tugged and prodded as if they didn't know my language or even my species, then seemed to have the sense to back off and let me stand. As soon as I was up they grabbed me and manhandled me pointlessly across the road. They threw me into the crowd. The first faces I saw were those of my brother Dominic and Tracy.

They'd both seen me and been worried. My brother urged me to stay calm and stay away from the police. Luckily my only injury was a small cut on my bottom lip which I had got as I fell. I knew I could cope with provocation and respond with calmness. I took a few breaths and felt fine. I was in a group of demonstrators, the noise level was up and there was tension as the police followed Soraya's violent arrest with more heavy-handedness. I stayed back.

A few yards away a police camera wielded by an Evidence Gatherer (E.G.) swept across the faces of the protesters, pointlessly recording their standing and waiting. It passed across me several times. In retrospect, what I did next left me exposed and gave them the option they needed. I took a few steps over to the camera and leaned forward. I wasn't that close. If the E.G. had extended his arm and I had reached out we probably still wouldn't have touched. I showed the mark on my lip, and said pointedly: "My lip, by your lot." Immediately I turned and walked off.

The E.G. had a minder, a snarling, unstable looking uniformed copper who looked as if he couldn't keep his temper when he was gardening. He marched after me shouting "Oi" or something similarly inarticulate. I turned back to see him catch up with me and just in time to see him move to prod me with a gloved hand. My hand went up in defence, and as the two hands touched, he was on me.

I lost all composure at once. There seemed to be several of them on me inside a second of our hands touching, and I lay face down. The weight of a knee on my back was enormous. Straight away I panicked. I screamed in pain, so they leaned harder.

The E.G's minder was leaning on me with his full weight, it seemed, which when concentrated on one knee made the pressure unbearable. I shouted that I couldn't breath. My chest was pressed hard against the tarmac. All I could move was my head, but they didn't let up at all. I said I wasn't resisting arrest, and felt a finger press in hard at the pressure point behind my ear as if that would shut me up. I shouted again that I wasn't resisting and would come easily, and they bent back my thumbs against the joint. I must have called out ten times, the violence, however, seemed to be a ritual part of the arrest.

Someone got hold of cuffs and locked them on my twisted arms. I heard a voice behind me calmly ask, "Do we really need all these police here?" My desperate optimism made me think for a second it might have been a senior police officer behaving rationally but it was another protester. The cuffs were on. I will never be persuaded that the design of the fixed handcuffs was for their superior restraining qualities rather than their infliction of pain. The fine edge cuts deep into the flesh and seldom leaves prisoners without bruises. Mine were far too tight.

At last the knee was taken from my back and I was able to breathe. Before it was fully off someone barked "Get up!" Broken as I was, I was determined to scramble to my feet, to avoid further attacks. It couldn't have been a second after the knee went that a copper grabbed my head lifting the only part I could move freely upwards and away from me, while the other held me back by my handcuffed wrists in a move to induce panic.[5]

Before I had managed to stand, a copper picked up my rucksack. It must have been knocked from my back when I was attacked, and had a plastic dog bowl, two litres of water for Eddy and little else. Before I was standing he hung the strap around my neck.

I shouted again that I was not resisting arrest and would come easily, but the original copper seemed to be in a frenzy now. He jerked my arm forward sending the pain from my wrist through my arms and barked "Come on." Holding my wrists up to maximise the pain he marched me over to the police van. They photographed me as I grimaced in pain.

After locking me in one van, I was moved to another. I stumbled in to see faces locked in each cell. Opposite me a dark haired women of about 30 looked dishevelled. More

---

5 Centre picture on page number 148.

usually involved in protests against live exports, she had been arrested for assaulting a police officer that was thirty yards behind her at the time. She was holding a floppy vegeburger, complete with salad etc. in each hand when she was supposed to have punched the policeman. She was disgusted with them. She started to mention something else that had happened during her arrest, then stopped talking about it; it was obviously something disturbing. Others in the van seemed to be randomly chosen. I found a "legal advice" leaflet in my pocket and read it out for everyone. I added that we were all entitled to a pen and paper, which I had already asked for five times, but was refused. Later I asked for it when I was processed at the police station, but was refused, even though I had them in front of me in my own property bag.

I was dragged up to the Magistrates four times, each was a complete waste of time and taxpayers' money. The charge of assaulting a police officer was dropped and re-placed by a public order offence. The arresting officer from Reading wrote a fanciful story that I had lunged at the cameraman, shouting insults, threats and expletives while he calmly asked me to stop. Eventually I grabbed his hand and twisted it, when he reluctantly arrested me. The police eventually did release the video, which showed the officer to be a liar, but the court case went on. At the time of writing, the court case against the police for assault and wrongful arrest has hit a stumbling block as the police deny it all, despite video evidence of the full event which proved the police witness statement utterly wrong and the arrest unacceptably heavy handed.

It will cost me a lot to take this further, and although I'm not rich I don't qualify for legal aid, so it seems our system of justice is shown to be one which allows extreme violence by known culprits to be used without question. Looking back I have no doubt that the arrest was an excuse to use an innocent bystander as a release of tension. Just as factory workers having bad days might thump their machines, or more, that day the police officer saw me as a convenient punch bag.

As time went on I heard more fanciful tales of arrests and violence from the Operation Stile cops and saw some shocking scenes firsthand. Years ago I would have expected a single incident like this to have led to disciplinary action and a serious review; now I know more about how the police work. Often following these smug attacks were snarled words like "You might be trying to close this farm, but I'm personally going to make sure it stays open."

Bad as my experience was on that day, I wouldn't have exchanged it with a Hill Grove cat on its best day. It was this realisation and others like it that kept me going.

Cris Iles

Chapter Thirteen

 **Campaign Trial**

*The police idea of remaining neutral is to beat you with their batons,
spray CS gas in your face repeatedly at close range, and then ask
questions.[1]*

Lynn and Cynthia, excluded from the demonstrations, would wait
on the one mile line ready to join in with chants and slogans as
soon as the marchers reached them. As soon as they saw the helicopter, they knew that the march was on the move. "You can ban
me from the farm. Keep me one mile away, but you can't stop me
now", Cynthia would shout at the police using a powerful new
megaphone. "Three cheers for the prisoners, Hip, hip hooray!
Brave men and women are put into prison by Thames Valley
Police." Three cheers again, louder than ever. The megaphone
was worth its weight in gold.

March 1998: Handing in a petition

ACT-AV had for some time been raising a petition and on the 5th
March 1998 it was handed it in to West Oxfordshire District
Council chairman, Mr Colin James. Marion Tyrrell[2], at 94 the
oldest campaigner, accompanied by Cynthia and other activists,
handed in the 11,000 signature petition for the closure of Hill

---

1 Laura.
2 Marion Tyrell died shortly after Hill Grove cat farm was shut down.

Grove farm, from a wheel chair. "I've lived through two world wars and I want to see us win this battle," 94-year-old Marion was reported saying[3]. The council, however, had a ready answer to the petition, telling the petitioners that the cat farm was a legal business and the council had no powers to close it down; so much for the voice of the people.

A trial for burglary

On the 9th March 1998 the trial began of Kievan Hickey, Brian Shiel, and Nichola Maddocks all charged with burglary at Hill Grove farm in January 1997. The case was expected to last about a week. Security at the court was strict and everyone who entered was searched. Brown arrived to give his evidence with a police escort. Inside the court the public gallery was full.

The defendants used their right to challenge jurors and managed to get four jurors to stand down after they stated that they had interests in either scientific research involving animals, the meat industry or hunting.

The prosecution case was that the three activists had broken into Hill Grove and stolen two boxes containing up to 18 kittens, as well as some breeding cats. Maddocks and Hickey had escaped with the stolen cats to the edge of the farm where the animals were passed to Shiel and other campaigners.

When the police arrived, however, the boxes were dropped and the protesters ran. The court heard that a ginger "breeding queen" called Margaret was stolen, as well as a cat called Zanny. When Hickey was arrested he was clutching a ginger cat which he refused to hand over to police officers.

The defence was aggressive, with the defendants claiming that Brown kept stolen cats for breeding. The defendants used the trial as an opportunity to make their case against Brown, his treat-

---

3 *Oxford Times*, March 6, 1998

ment of cats and their sale for vivisection. Brown in his evidence claimed that he was not cruel to the cats nor did he have anything to do with stolen cats,[4] it was he said, "absolutely atrocious that anybody would suggest it." At one stage in the trial a box that was used to send cats to the labs was displayed.[5] Gasps went up. Cynthia let out a cry of "Dreadful", and was ticked off by the judge with the words, "Madam, any more of this and you will have to leave. This is a court of law."

Cross-examination by the defence counsel managed to dig out some information about the regime at Hill Grove.[6] The staff at the farm made all the breeding records and the Home Office neither kept records nor carried out inspections. Kittens were all tattooed at 8 weeks old with tattoo pliers. Ink was punched into the tissue of the ear. The kittens were not given anaesthetic for this.

The defence cross examined about a cat called Margaret, a ginger breeding queen, which was returned to Brown on January 18th 1997. Brown had told the police, before the cats were recovered that all the cats had tattoos on their ears but Margaret had no tattoo. Unfortunately, Brown said, Margaret was now dead. Despite being an exhibit in the case, she had been "culled" just two weeks before the trial. Brown said all breeding queens at Hill Grove farm were culled at 10 years of age. There was "nothing sinister about Margaret being culled. She came to the end of her breeding life."

The defence made much of the fact that there was a very high number of deaths in new born kittens at Hill Grove. Brown agreed that their own mothers killed 10% of kittens. A list was read out in court from Brown's own records. "Page 4: Kittens eaten, bitten through stomach, Page 7: Seven kittens eaten, bitten

---

4 *Oxford Mail*, March 10, 1998.
5 It was learned that the box, one and a half foot by two, had gauze-type air filters and the cat would be confined in complete darkness.
6 The following account of evidence given at the court case, is taken mainly from the campaign newsletter written by Heather James.

through back; Page 11: Broke neck (mother broke her kitten's neck); Page 15: Kittens strangled by umbilical cord, broken back legs; Page 33: Bitten through head; Page 34: Eaten up to neck; Page 34: All kittens eaten; Page 38: Ripped head open."

The defence said that they had learned from experts that the only reason for queens eating or damaging their kittens were excessive stress and the fact that they sensed danger. Two workers at Hill Grove claimed that they did not know where the cats went when they left the farm. On cross-examination, one worker said that the breeding queens were put into stud pens with approximately eight other queens and one tom. When the queen was obviously heavily pregnant she was removed and put into the "flats" to have her kittens. When the kittens were eight weeks old were removed, tattooed and the queens returned to the stud pen.

A couple of days before the end of the trial, it was announced that Brown had been attacked by masked men, this publicity was seen by campaigners as a move to influence the jury.[7] When the trial concluded Kievan Hickey was found guilty and received 12 months imprisonment; the other defendants were adquitted.

People were now coming from far afield to support the campaign, coaches came from Scotland and individuals came from other European countries. As the demonstrations continued, all vehicles coming into the area were stopped and protesters searched. In March 1998, rocks were thrown through the windows of Cynthia O'Neill's house. Cynthia's son Brendan was quickly on his feet and gave chase to the two youths whom he saw running from the premises. One of the culprits dropped his bag of large rocks. The police were decidedly uninterested in investigating this harassment.

---

7 *The Oxford Mail* reported that Christopher Brown was attacked in the centre of Witney as he tried to remove a poster calling for his cat-breeding centre to be closed. Mr Brown, who has vowed not to let protesters put him out of business, was quoted in the *Mail* as saying: "This is the sort of people these protesters are, a load of thugs. It is illegal to put posters up like this, yet they disagree with people taking them down. This has increased my determination to keep my business going." *The Oxford Mail* March 20, 1998.

A specific technical breach in a general quagmire of wrong [8]

I am a professionally qualified animal technician. During the 90s I have worked with cats and with Specific Pathogen Free (SPF) animals in research laboratories. It is claimed that the cats at Hill Grove farm are Specific Pathogen Free animals.

Following an attempted release of cats from Hill Grove, it came out in the court case that the cats which had escaped to the outside world were immediately returned to their sheds. This is clearly a breach of SPF conditions.

If cats had made it to the wrong room within the building, e.g. a staff room or changing room, they would be considered contaminated. Their return to the colony would also lead to the loss of SPF status of any cats coming into contact with the escapees.

The SPF label which Hill Grove had was offered by the Laboratory Animals Breeders Association. This body is composed entirely of directors and secretaries from companies which breed animals for experiments.

It is hard to believe an attitude of "you scratch my back and I'll scratch yours" has not developed in such a group. Certainly my professional experience of the industry showed me what a closed, incestuous group business animal experiments are.

But does it really matter? SPF cats are appalling models for human illnesses and injury, as are all animals. Their reaction to treatment differs wildly from ours. The same is true of non-SPF animals.

The cruelty inflicted and the time wasted gaining useless results from animal experiments that I have witnessed makes the police bill for Hill Grove demonstrations seem relatively minor.

---

8 This letter appeared in *The Standard* August 18, 1998 and in the *Oxford Mail* August 19, 1998.

Chapter Fourteen

🐈 The Police Lose It

> *The police completely lost control and were just charging on horseback at people that weren't even doing anything. One elderly man fell and my friend tried to help him to his feet but was punched in the face by the police.*[1]

Around 3,000 campaigners attended the protest outside Hill Grove farm on Saturday 18th April 1998. During the battle that followed, there were a number of casualties and ten arrests. Long, hard months of planning, adverts in the *Big Issue*, posters and the linking of the demonstration to World Day for Lab Animals encouraged a large attendance.

It was truly a battle. The noise of the helicopter, police dogs barking, activists protesting louder than ever, megaphones bellowing out and the commands of agitated and worried police ranks. One activist counted five ambulances called to the scene to deal with the unarmed but wounded activists.

From a Shoreham protester[2]

That day at the farm, yes you all know the one, when the roof went. I stood in the field watching a row of riot police with their backs towards the house. Down at the end

---

1 Heather James, spokeswoman for *Save the Hill Grove Cats*.
2 Sadly Cone Bill, a truly great character who we were privileged to have known and who always travelled with the Shoreham contingent, died in late 1999.

against Dry Lane the mounted police waited. Stones started to rain on the house from the crowd. Who started it?

We've since heard stories of police agents provocateur seen later in the car park. The stones continued to rain down, but the police didn't move. The electricity lines sparked and tiles cascaded. The mounted police moved slowly up the field towards us and then turned and moved back.

Why weren't they making any attempt to stop the damage? The stones continued. Then they all moved in and broke up the crowd. What where their motives for waiting so long? It all became clear some time later when they started arresting people they'd picked out on their numerous cameras.

One question has never been answered satisfactorily: Is it the job of the police to stand by and watch a crime being committed so that they can arrest the greatest number of people at a later date or is it their job to prevent a crime from happening? After all, if someone smashes a jeweller's shop window the police don't stand by and let everyone steal the goods from the window, hoping to arrest them all later, do they?

Manna from Heaven

Rose's arrest was inevitable. She had written and demonstrated on behalf of the campaign. She was thrown face down on the ground with both her hands handcuffed behind her back and left in the hot sun.

She was in Brown's back garden and could see the tiles still falling from the farmhouse roof. The helicopter was making a dreadful noise, almost it seemed down amongst the demonstrators. Police dogs barked incessantly, arrest vans tore around as the demonstrators chanted: "Come out and show yourself Brown, come on out and tell us where those cats go."

Rose's handcuffs cut into her wrists. She could see another prisoner in the same situation. Shocked and stunned she was kept trussed up in the sun unable to move and given extra punishment as she refused to give her name and address, a refusal to which she was perfectly entitled. She heard the police calling for reinforcements and receive the news that there were none!

Rose tried hard not to cry, to be a coward, or let the animals down in any way. She was also determined not to shout abuse at the cops. She lay there baking in the heat, her wrists bleeding. She was shaken and of course frightened. Soon, there was no feeling in her thumb and first two fingers of each hand. Still trussed up, she was put, half sitting, in a hot, stuffy police van.

A sympathetic Hants police officer saw her distressed state. The van door was tightly closed and then the man's kind soft voice offered her some water and helped her hold the plastic cup and drink. With other prisoners Rose was driven, a bumpy ride, to Newbury police station, the HQ for "Operation Stile" to be interrogated and eventually charged with "violent disorder".

The driver of the riot van was the kind Hampshire officer and, looking over that terrible day's events, did Rose imagine a look in the officer's eyes as much as to say "I'm truly sorry. We have two cats at home and you could be my own daughter. I wish I had the guts to do what you and your friends have done today. I am truly sorry." Or was it just in Rose's imagination?

Medieval Warfare

There was an occasion when I witnessed protesters make a breach with a tree trunk or long beam in a metal perimeter wall. Behind the wall were police who appeared with their shields over their heads like the Roman "testudo" military formation, and then a squad of mounted police came cantering around the corner. Everyone cheered and jeered.

The scene reminded me of pictures of medieval warfare with one army seeking to enter a walled city while missiles rain down on them from the ramparts. But here the missiles sometimes bounced back onto the heads of the assailants if they failed to clear the top of the metal wall, so that I saw one young man, with blood streaming down his face, being helped away from the scene of the battle by his companions after being hit with a missile.

Henry Turtle

After the Battle

Casualties of the battle included a young boy who was bumped by a police horse, a 34 year old man who was treated at the John Radcliffe for a suspected heart attack, a 48 year old man who broke his hip falling from a tree and a 63 year old man who was knocked unconscious when a police riot shield was allegedly thrust at him. One young man lost a finger, amputated after a rock thrown from the direction of the police lines hit his hand. No police officers suffered serious injuries.

While the police began an investigation based on video footage and intelligence gathered during the demonstration, with the aim of arresting more people, the first seven arrested were released on conditional bail to appear before Witney Magistrates Court. A further three people were bailed to reappear at Newbury Police Station.

At the end of the demonstration, an activist noticed people in the crowd who had allegedly been seen throwing missiles and encouraging others to cause damage to the fencing and house, taking off their "activists outfits", and having changed into police cadet uniforms climb into a police van.

Rose and other activists spent some hours locked in police cells before release. The police doctor who examined Rose found she had thirty-one lacerations to her body, including wrists, thigh, legs and arms. Rose still has a scar on her left wrist where the handcuffs cut her. When she began to sue the police, all the police doctor's notes went 'missing'. Not the first time evidence effecting the campaign had been 'lost'.

In the aftermath of the battle, campaigners were left to ruefully consider the fact that had their been more protesters present that day the cats would probably have been liberated. They had come so close to moving onto the farm by sheer force of numbers.

Long after the last demonstrator had left the scene, six Thames Valley police stood in front of their riot van blocking the entrance to Hill Grove farm, with fluorescent yellow jacket uniforms catching the glow of passing car headlights. As if guarding a site of great symbolic importance, they stood ready to shine their torches and long distance infrared beams on passing cars and motorists. High above the scene of the recent tumult, thick night clouds gathered before a gentle April moon filtering a silvery quiet over the site. It had been a very hard day but the campaigners could say that they had given their best.

Chapter Fifteen

🐈 A Turn of the Screw

If amid the din and clatter of the devil's workshop one true note is sounded, our besotted memory stirs itself – our dull wits wake to listen.[1]

A 100,000 signature petition collected by Save the Hill Grove Cats was handed into the Home Office in Swindon on the 19th May 1998. In the best tradition of British democracy, Home Office officials refused to accept it and called the police. How many times had the campaigners been told "Use the proper channels?"

The Hill Grove campaign newsletter number six appeared in colour for the first time and showed a picture of four kittens saved from Hill Grove. The four 6-week-old kittens had been rescued after they had been put in a vehicle ready for despatch to a lab when activists entered the farm. A woman chained herself to a car steering wheel in an attempt to block the entrance to Hill Grove farm. In May campaigners protested at Pan Air, a Colchester livestock transport company and against Oxford University Physiology Department.[2] Throughout May everyone organised for another major demonstration to be held at the end of the

---

1 Robert Blatchford. Fantasias. Cited in *Robert Blatchford: The Sketch of a Personality: An estimate of some achievements.* A. Neil Lyons. The Clarion Press. 1910. An account of the famous socialist, newspaper creator, journalist, pamphleteer and novelist.
2 *The Oxford Mail,* May 27, 1998.

month. Thirty nine demonstrators, including a ten year old boy, were arrested during this demonstration.[3] The police used the opportunity of the demonstration to arrest people they had targeted during the last demonstration.

As he had done on other occasions, the Rev. James Thompson, 68, a retired rector and a former senior hospital chaplain in Aberdeen, gave a service for the campaigners and the animals. He later told the *Oxford Mail*: "I feel the church, which claims to be the moral mouthpiece of the nation, should be taking a stand against cruelty." "This is comparable to the slave trade a couple of hundred years ago. It's our task as Christians to protect life."

A Frustrating but Valuable Involvement

As we travelled in the mini-bus we had plenty of time to think about tomorrow and what it would bring! I had planned this journey for a long time since I first learnt about Hill Grove farm. One could not even visualise the horrors that the cats would have to endure at the hands of man.

A fairly large group of us from Edinburgh had got together and organised a trip down, travelling overnight in both directions. No doubt we all had our private thoughts and feelings about the demo. Although there was no doubt that we would be peaceful, we were determined to show people there is no place in society for such treatment of animals.

We had several stops on the way, which brought some respite from our cramped conditions in the mini-bus. It was a fine dry night, ideal for driving. We arrived outside Oxford at a motorway cafe and were met by Cynthia. She had everything organised including breakfast, which some of us desperately needed. After freshening up we all felt

---

3 *Oxford Mail*, June 1, 1998.

ready for anything! A cup of tea always gives that feeling! We took photos, got ourselves ready and followed Cynthia in her car to the meeting point at the Leys. We were amongst the first to arrive.

Shortly afterwards all sorts of people arrived in various forms of transport. It was a nice dry and sunny morning which lifted spirits sky high and believe me, when you saw the army of police all wearing riot gear, we needed it! I have never seen so many police in my life, quite a few on horseback. A lady constable on a very friendly horse spoke to me. She seemed interested to hear about our side. Initially, the whole atmosphere was of a convivial nature, peaceful and friendly. The atmosphere changed when several speakers got onto a small platform to speak on behalf of the animals.

The police helicopter flew so low over us we couldn't hear a thing and we realised the police were doing this on purpose. I had met Celia Hammond whilst walking around, another caring lady for the campaign, who has herself raised funds for her own animal sanctuary and animal hospital. Then it was time to move off for the walk to Hill Grove. Everyone was peaceful, chatting and determined to do their bit.

A few locals showed disapproval but many showed encouragement. The police were everywhere, with arms linked across the road; goodness knows what they thought we were going to do. Some were very intimidating in their manner. Eventually we got near Hill Grove but the police would not let us up near the farm, so we simply rested. The police then decided they wanted to go home and the trouble began; they lost their heads! All hands joined, they herded us into a group on three sides and tried to herd us like cattle.

I felt so hot, stuck in the crowd, being pushed, I asked a policewoman "Can I have some air?" No reply, and then I was shoved and down I went. My friend got me up and out. It was frightening, since I felt I would have been trodden on if I had not been saved.

Our walk back was escorted by police vans; safety in numbers no doubt! I said to one policeman that at least with them accompanying us, we wouldn't be attacked, but his sense of humour was missing -not even a smile. It was frustrating not getting to the farm, but we had made our presence felt. The trip gave us all a lot to think about.

On the 2nd June 1998, the **Sorted** page in the *Daily Mirror* published an expose which gave all the campaigners a lift. Entitled, What's going on at Mr Brown's cat farm? A colour photograph showed an angry Christopher Brown claiming that the very documents on which the article was based had in fact been taken from his farm.

Chapter Sixteen

ϗ On Trial Again

I hope you can live with yourselves. You'll have this on your conscience for the rest of your lives. How can you fine me for my right to protest? I'd rather go to prison.[1]

On Thursday 11th June 1998, Cynthia O'Neill was before the court for the third time, this time Oxford Crown Court. Charged with harassment, Cynthia appeared fearless in the face of the many obstacles and threats that the police and the State threw at her. From an ordinary retired Queen's Nursing Sister living quietly in Oxfordshire, Cynthia had become a seasoned protester for whom neither the police, nor the courts held any threat or social stigma.

> Tuning into my car radio, on the way to court beautiful Handel organ music was being played. But what happiness can there ever be for me when I'm haunted by the lab animals night and day? Tears streamed down my face again. "Dear Lord, please take away their suffering. Don't let them suffer too much." I was forced to turn the music off.

Cynthia had become conscious of the fact that a campaign of this kind needed good solicitors and barristers to fight their cases. They needed a legal team that would take every opportunity to state their case and argue for the right to demonstrate. Outside the court, friends gathered.

---

1 Cynthia O'Neill reported in *The Guardian*, June 12, 1998.

On occasions like this, Cynthia thought of herself acting for the lab animals and considered it her duty to do her best, including using every word she said to its utmost effect. Before entering the court at half past nine, Rev. James Thompson gave her his blessing. Cynthia didn't feel hopeful, considering that most Magistrates court findings are a foregone conclusion. The words 'proper channels' kept coming into her mind; all she had been doing was speaking through a megaphone.

Brown took a diary to court and referred to a catalogue of incidents over a six-month period. He said O'Neill shouted at and abused him, sometimes using a megaphone, at his farm and in Witney town centre. Cynthia's defence counsel, Kevin Tomlinson, said that there was no evidence that she has ever threatened Mr Brown. She had only shouted at him, sometimes with a megaphone.

Predictably Cynthia was found guilty, fined £50 plus £75 costs and a further restriction order was placed on her. The proceedings were a complete waste of public money. She told the court that she would go to prison rather than pay the fine. She didn't, however, have the choice because friends and colleagues immediately paid her fine. After the hearing, she decided that it was politically expedient as well as just and right to pursue the conviction to Appeal.

The day following her trial when the newspapers might have been expected to carry a fair report of her conviction, *The Oxford Times* carried the following item:

> Animal rights extremists have renewed their campaign against the cat breeder, Mr Chris Brown, and the Oxford Professor, Colin Blakemore, with letter bombs posted to their homes. Further devices were posted to two workers at Mr Brown's farm. Police, who described the incidents as "cowardly attacks", said all four victims escaped unhurt after realising the packages were suspicious. Army bomb experts were brought in to deal with the packages, which were delivered on Tuesday.[2]

---

2 *The Oxford Times,* June 12, 1998.

Assistant Chief Constable Robert Davies said: "These letters had got the potential to cause serious injury to the recipient, and it is important that members of the public are vigilant and do not hesitate to contact the police if they receive any suspicious packages."

Chapter Seventeen

🐈 RSPCA Endorses Brown

*We have always maintained an impartial view about the farm's
activities and have worked hard to keep a balance between people's
right to protest and the right of Mr Brown to run a lawful business.*[1]

June 20th 1998

On learning that Prof. Blakemore was giving a lecture in St Mary
Radcliffe Church in Bristol, in June 1998, Cynthia wasted no time
travelling there with Victoria Plum. Bristol was after all, well
beyond Cynthia's one mile Hill Grove exclusion order. Arriving
at the church, they were met by two riot vans and six officers,
who, after the audience had been treated to Cynthia's brave and
withering invective, escorted them from the church.

A signed cheque, on the dashboard of a worker's car leaving
Hill Grove farm, informed the campaign that Christopher Brown
banked with Lloyd's. Cynthia's next target was the manager of
Lloyds Bank, Witney. She visited the bank on several occasions
before a final showdown with the manager in the bank foyer.

"Do you mind leaving? You're upsetting the customers," the
manager said.

"Good, let them know, you are either a part of the solution
or a part of the problem," said Cynthia.

---

1 Asst. Chief Con. Robert Davies of Thames Valley Police.

"I shall call the police," the bank manager threatened.

"Please do, I'm not frightened and I'm not committing an offence."

Determined to get her money's worth and knowing the police station was only around the corner, Cynthia addressed the customers loudly: "Lloyds Bank take money from cat breeder Brown. Blood money, money from vivisection."

Cynthia continued with a variation on this theme until she knew she had to go. Just in time, as she drove away, the TVP came rushing up the High Street. As she drove away she said out loud: "Missed the culprit! Tough luck. She's quicker than you think."

Park and Demonstrate. Oxford City Centre

The campaign's July demonstration due to march through Witney, was banned by the police with the backing of Jack Straw, the Home Secretary. The excuse was given that it would clash with Witney's annual carnival, which was being held in the same area.

As they had done in the past, campaign organisers thought quickly and moved the whole demonstration from "Pear Tree Park and Ride," where it had assembled, to the Centre of Oxford. One campaigner had already been arrested in Witney, before the demonstration, for putting up arrow signs to direct people to the field next to the Leys so Hill Grove's rally would not interfere with the carnival. He was later released without charge.

Splitting up the march caused the police maximum confusion. Over five hundred marchers made for the Oxford University Department of Physiology and as traffic came to a standstill police tried to block their way. Some of the marchers moved to the north Oxford home of physiology professor Colin Blakemore. Fifteen demonstrators were arrested during the day.

An Adaptable Organism

A full coach left Brighton at 8.30 for Witney to demonstrate at Hill Grove farm. The day started off warm and dry but we were promised wind and heavy rain in the afternoon. We were all in fairly good spirits in the hope that closure of the breeders was perhaps nearer than it was last month!

We were about 10 miles from Witney when we heard that the police had put up a 5-mile exclusion zone around the town! The rumour was confirmed when we came to a roadblock where police were diverting anyone they thought might be demonstrating into a lay-by. We were informed that we would not be allowed any further; anyone that tried to pass would be arrested. Apparently the application had been made by the police to the County Council with Jack Straw's support.

The police were acting under the 1986 Public Order Act brought in by Thatcher conveniently in time for the miners' strike.[2] People got off the coach and some held up their placards so that other motorists could see what was happening, and what Hill Grove was participating in. It was overheard that the police were going to make an arrest of one of our people who was still on the coach. Several police officers and a WPC entered the coach pushing aside people, they then arrested a female protester for an alleged incident at a previous demonstration.

When people started to ask questions the police told them to "Mind your own business, it's got nothing to do with you." Another of the demonstrators tried to follow the police in an attempt to find out exactly what was happening. This protester was roughly pushed aside and was subjected to a search under S60; all because they dared to ask questions!

---

2 Used against the miners to stop them picketing and against the Stonehenge protesters to stop them gathering.

We were told to board the coach and go home! They obviously don't know us very well. Through various channels we found out where everyone was to meet. If we couldn't demonstrate in Witney, then we would have a demonstration elsewhere.

At a service station just outside Oxford, cars, vans and coaches converged; this seemed a good place to start. We would let the people of Oxford know what was going on in the little town of Witney, 15 miles away. The crowd started to walk into Oxford. The police were totally unprepared for this and mass panic could be seen in their ranks. Police cars, vans and bikes suddenly appeared, lights flashing and sirens blaring, after the march had travelled about three quarters of a mile along a very busy main road.

It was along this section of the road that a young demonstrator was hit by a vehicle, tossed onto the bonnet of the car and then thrown off onto the road. The police who were present did not attempt to stop this vehicle, it drove off leaving a young man lying injured in the road. An ambulance was called and the injured person was taken to hospital.

The march pressed on. The road was blocked, with the help of the police, and the traffic was building up for as far as we could see. The march continued, the demonstrators outwitting the police by turning into residential side roads, to a chant of "close down Hill Grove farm." Residents were in no doubt as to the reason why people were marching *en masse*.

Turning back onto a main road, the marchers stopped at a shopping centre, the road was blocked and the chants went on. Speakers on loud hailers let the surrounding shops and people know of the vivisection industry. The reaction from stranded motorists was good. People generally asked us questions and were not annoyed at being held up by our demonstration. Very few disagreed with our views.

Two police helicopters arrived, and we could hear and then see police horses cantering along the road to confront us. The usual heavy-handed louts, safe on horseback, had arrived to support their foot-colleagues. Their usual strategy came into force after a short period, firstly blocking our way and then using the horses to push us wherever they wanted. They have no regard for their horses, they use them as they would use their batons: as public order tools.

They had on their spurs and it was noticed that one horse had a bad wound on its flanks. This was pointed out and ignored. What can you say? Several people were arrested, no doubt the police were able to find something to charge them with.

The rain started to fall quite heavily and the demonstration got very wet. The roads had been blocked in various places for over three hours so it was decided to move back to the service station. We thought that a wave by all the demonstrators to the police helicopter hovering above was in order, so to a loud shout all hands went up in the air to wave. What a scene!

We proceeded to walk back to the parked vehicles. About half a mile from the service station we came to a large roundabout with major roads off, one being a dual carriageway. Deciding that a walk would be a fitting end to the day, we did half an hour's worth around the roundabout. The police stood back and blocked every junction.

Drivers were now getting annoyed, wanting the police to move us on; some sat with their hands on hooters, and were politely told by demonstrators to "shut it." The heavy brigade decided that enough was enough and the horses were ridden at the marchers, while the forces on the ground started pushing and shoving in no uncertain terms. Anyone who did not move, mainly because they couldn't, was pulled out and arrested. One young lad was grabbed by four officers, pushed to the ground and was seen to be kicked by police. When people tried to video this event the police closed ranks and shielded what was going on.

People were threatened with arrest for trying to film the situation, and one very red faced officer, with watering glazed eyes was told to calm down and get himself together by a protester. This made him even angrier and the protester had to move quickly to avoid arrest by the madman!

The police obviously thought that because they had got an exclusion zone, signed by the Home Office, we would all go home disappointed. They didn't know us then, did they? By their actions they actually brought a lot more attention to our cause. We could not have hoped to reach so many people in a few hours. *Thank you for your help Thames Valley police.*

The RSPCA strikes again; August 1998

In July another massive collection of signatures, 200,000 this time, was handed in at the Home Office in London. More questions were being asked about the soaring costs to the public purse, defending Brown's business. Costs for policing now stood at around £750,000. The Green Party suggested scaling it down.

Following parliamentary pressure, in June, Maggy Jennings of the Research Animals Department of the RSPCA went to Hill Grove farm accompanied by two RSPCA Inspectors, to report on the conditions in which the cats were kept. After the visit, she told the campaign that Brown had been given prior notice of the "inspection" and denied them access to the breeding sheds so they had only viewed the cats through a glass screen.

Jennings wrote to RSPCA council members before her report was made, saying: "I can say that none of us saw any evidence of cruelty or mistreatment of the cats, or anything that conflicts with existing legislation or codes of practice, other than that which we already knew from the Home Office (i.e. some of the pens are slightly below the new size requirements)."

Jennings also said: "Our concerns are those that we would have in any breeding situation, for example, the frequency of pregnancies and lifetime confinement even when the pens are large." These were exactly the issues brought up in the trial of Hill Grove activists. In that trial breeding records were referred to. "Members of the public have sent us copies of the breeding records from Hill Grove farm. These have been examined by our professional veterinary staff who consider that they do not reveal evidence of cruel treatment."

Rather than address the much larger question of selling live animals for vivisection, the RSPCA focused on the idea of what the regulations allowed and on the apparent welfare of the cats. This meant that they didn't have to answer the question of whether it was cruel to breed cats for experiment, or whether vivisection was cruel, nor did they have anything to say about breeding continuously, or keeping queens imprisoned for the duration of their whole life, or weaning kittens before they were eight weeks old.

The campaigners were stunned when they heard that the RSPCA had found nothing wrong in the breeding records. Save the Hill Grove Cats was all about preventing the suffering of the cats and its ultimate goal was to shut Hill Grove down. But in the interim the campaign had hoped that the cats would be kept in the best possible conditions. The cats were not kept in good conditions, they were overcrowded, stressed and exhausted and they never saw the light of day.

Cynthia raises money

Cynthia used to say: "Not having any money trees in my garden, it often fell to me to fundraise. You can at the end of the day, only depend on yourself." Fundraising is an essential part of campaigning, not to be seen as something peripheral. Cynthia saw fundraising, especially at car boot sales, as a way of propagandising the struggle and of getting about and meeting people.

On her way to do a stamp fair to raise much needed funds, Cynthia was invited to meet a remarkable seventy-eight year old, active campaigner. On opening her door, she knew she was one of them. Boxes of jumble, books, leaflets, and as in Cynthia's house, a beautifully decorated loo, so friends could sit for the day and cogitate ways to stop vivisection! "Why not?" Cynthia said, "We have our priorities right."

One hot Sunday afternoon, Natasha called to see Cynthia and found her surrounded by empty aluminium cans, foil dishes etc. "Watcha"... What on earth... ?" she said. Due to the heat Cynthia had on a flimsy dress and was busy beating the cans with one of her walking sticks and stamping on them to flatten them. Natasha was non-plussed coming across what appeared to be an ethnic Oxford war dance. The wasps seemed to like the remnants of beer in the cans so Cynthia was being careful, occasionally stepping off the job to escape them.

Pointing to the three full sacks, Cynthia said: "£6 on that lot, not bad is it?" Natasha, who quickly got into the swing of things helped to finish the fourth sack. "Eight pounds in all, each empty aluminium can will fetch half a penny and the £8 will fund 800 leaflets."

Two more protesters were sent to prison. Judge Anthony King was now doling out tougher jail sentences. Non-animal activists would rarely get prison for a first offence with a clean record. Campaigner Jacob Saunders was awarded £400 for wrongful arrest -he donated every penny to the campaign.

September 1998 demonstration through Witney town centre

The Scots came again for another demo. This time they had a slightly more comfortable coach. John Cowen had raised a great deal of money for the campaign from his stalls and letters. Their buses, cars and vans were all searched by police as they entered the Witney area.

The demonstration was again subject to an exclusion order stopping it from going near Hill Grove farm. After a rally on the edge of Witney, about 1,000 demonstrators marched through Witney town centre. Police arrested 15 protesters for offences including assault and criminal damage.

Following this march, in September Thames Valley Police Chief Constable Charles Pollard made his unintentionally funny statement about the protesters. "Hill Grove farm protesters could disappear like New Age travellers," he said, "Take the concept of New Age travellers, it just suddenly went. They stopped because the police became very good at policing them."[4]

Cynthia's choral work

On learning that Christchurch Cathedral, Oxford, was to be the venue for 50 years thanksgiving for the NHS, Cynthia decided to take the message about lab animals there. Wearing her white T-shirt emblazoned with "Vivisection is Scientific Fraud" she grabbed the opportunity to focus on the matter of a health care system still based on fraudulent animal research.

Following the bidding prayer by the Rev. R. Jeffery, Sub Dean of Christchurch, she seized the silence, standing and shouting: "No wonder there is so much chronic ill-health. More than one in ten patients in hospital are there with illnesses caused by animal 'safety tested' drugs. For over 50 years animals and stolen pets have been abused in these hospital vivisection labs. In 1998, yes 50 years on, our health care is still based on fraudulent animal research."

Perched, as she was, at the front of the cathedral, Cynthia was "led out" the full length of the church by the clergy, one of whom put his hands over her mouth! Despite the fact that she

---

4 *Oxford Mail,* September 8, 1998.

needed it to walk, they took her walking frame from her. Despite their most un-Christian methods Cynthia continued: "No animal is a model for man," walking as slowly as possible to get every penny's worth. She was rewarded by one lady who winked in approval from the pews. "No good will ever come from evil. Close all the vivisection labs in the Oxford Hospitals today, and with the money keep open our much needed Wallingford, Burford and Witney hospitals." Near the exit she managed to get in: "Vivisection is barbaric, useless and a hindrance to medical progress. Dr Hartinger, Chief Surgeon, Germany 1988."

At the church doors, the strong hands of the police fell on her: "Oxford, the city of sin, the city of vivisection." "You should be ashamed of yourself," cried a senior cleric. "You should all be ashamed of vivisection," she responded. The door were nearly shut behind her with her final words: "Trust the church to support vivisection with shares in Viagra!" The door was shut tight and an interview with the police followed. "Anything you say will be taken down in evidence, blah, blah, blah," Cynthia mimicked later, "I had my money's worth! I didn't hurt anyone. Got them thinking. The acoustics were beautiful."

From Scotland

As an animal lover I was always against animal abuse whatever form it took. My pet hate is vivisection. Along with millions of others I agreed with Gandhi that vivisection was the vilest evil of all. As far as I was concerned this was particularly true when cats were the victims. I was therefore glad when I was put into contact with the Hill Grove campaign. I fully approve of their actions in bringing farmer Brown's business to the notice of the public.

Some well-meaning animal lovers disapproved of the activities preferring to go through the official channels. But those of us who have travelled down that road know how frustrating and heartbreaking it is. It is soul destroying to be either ignored or receive the same stereotyped waffle others were receiving no matter what you wrote. Every ignored letter or stereotyped waffle reply only made me more determined to carry on and support the Hill Grove campaign.

I first met Cynthia when she was on trial for harassment of farmer Brown at Oxford Sheriff Court on the 11th June 1998. From the first she struck me as a very dedicated campaigner who would stop at nothing to end the hell of vivisection. Not for her the softly, softly measures of the standard so-called animal protection societies. She was a thorn in the side of farmer Brown and his lackeys, the police. The trial itself was typical and resulted in Cynthia being banned from the vicinity of Hill Grove farm. She was given the ultimatum of paying a total fine of £150 or go to prison. Cynthia said she would not pay and would rather go to prison.

Those of us present in court persuaded her not to by raising the cash amongst ourselves to prevent this. Of course many others have gone through similar ordeals and have either been heavily fined or ended up in prison. Such set backs only made us more determined to continue.

The campaign attracted ever-growing support. Coaches came from all over the United Kingdom. The Scottish contingent was present at most of them. We travelled complete with flags, banners etc. Cynthia met us at the Little Chef for a talk and an exchange of information. Soon after we left Cynthia to complete the last leg of our journey, we were stopped by the Flying Squad who ordered us out while our coach and persons were searched. In time this became a standard joke particularly as the police never found the bombs or offensive weapons they were obviously looking for. So much for the anarchist and violent terrorist hysteria whipped up by the media at the behest of the Government and the commercial profiteers, backers of the vivisectors. Each demo had its highlights, particularly the ones when the fence and Brown's house were stormed.

One of the foremost niggles throughout the campaign was the complete lack of support from the orthodox societies who, it appeared, were loath to be associated with the tactics of the campaigners, notwithstanding the fact that their own weak efforts to persuade the Home Office to close Hill Grove and take more effective action against vivisection generally were doomed to failure. The RSPCA in the person of Maggy Jennings claimed that no cruelty existed at Hill Grove despite all the well vetted documentation produced. Jennings based this on being allowed to view proceedings through a small and totally inadequate window.

A member of the Animal Welfare Advisory Committee did not advise the Home Office to close Hill Grove, the same stance was taken in regard to Porton Down, Shamrock monkeys and Huntingdon, etc. The church does not seem to recognise or accept that animals are God's creations and not put on earth to be tortured, abused or killed for commercial profit or so called sport. Despite this background our tactics were vindicated. But as said before, there is still a long, long way to go before the final victory is won.

John Cowen

Oxford Courier Newspapers

De-describing
boundaries

Hill Grove
Farm

Witney

Oxford Courier Newspapers

If it takes five police officers to
arrest one demonstrator and a
megaphone how many...

Oxford Courier Newspapers

Front line

Hill Grove

News Team International

I used to play rugby league..

Oxford Courier Newspapers

Police camouflaged using bovine waste material

Hill Farm 'I tell you he's one of ours'

Witney

Campaign picture

A good talking to

Oxford Courier Newspapers

A manifestation
of feeling

Hill Grove

HILLGROVE
CLOSED
HOORAY!

Victory!

Campaign picture

Campaign picture

Lucy and Tilbey two of the 800 rescued cats

Chapter Eighteen

🐈 I Just Wish I Could See a Future!

It's a terrible step down the path towards anarchy if a business can be closed down by a small group of misinformed activists.[1]

While Christopher Brown told the newspapers that his future was diminishing, the campaigners sensed theirs expanding. While Brown was, in his own words "cheesed off", most of the campaigners had been cheesed off for years with vivisectors and their disregard for animal life.

In September 1998, both the *Independent* and the *Oxford Mail* published articles that criticised the campaign and exhorted campaigners to throw in the towel. "Showdown on the farm"[2] a lengthy article, worth reading for what Richard Aswith failed to say, stirred questions from both sides. Several people phoned and faxed the *Independent* asking for corrections. Why was it that some of the media never gave the campaigner's side of the picture? The editor of the *Oxford Mail* exasperated with the letters flooding onto his desk, suggested the campaign call it a day[3] and closed his letter page. "The Hill Grove cat farm issue has now occupied countless column inches in "Our Say" for the past few months. Unless some new argument or development comes to light, correspondence on this emotive subject is now closed –Editor."

1 Christopher Brown.
2 *The Independent* September 5, 1998.
3 *Oxford Mail* September 17,1998.

The enemy was always looking for ammunition to change hearts and minds against the campaign. In September the *Independent* got Stephen Hawkins on side as a journalist and social commentator. A Nobel Prize winning scientist, known to the public primarily for presenting a television advertisement with his artificially generated voice, Hawkins supported Blakemore and condemned the Hill Grove campaigners.

Cynthia Appeals

On the 2nd of October at Oxford Crown Court Cynthia appealed her conviction for 'harassment'. It was a whitewash. Like everything else that took place in the courts, the appeal was a strategy, the only channel available, so it had to be used to maximum effect. Although Cynthia had recently been in hospital on a number of occasions and was quite unwell, she still wanted to fight.

The police knew that there was a good chance that Cynthia might win the case because it had not been proved at the first hearing that she had been causing harassment; Brown had even agreed that she might not have been harassing him. Both the police and Christopher Brown were well prepared for this next round against Cynthia. Their information about Cynthia and her megaphone differed from that presented at the first hearing.

To avoid any chance of a victory for Cynthia, the police brought new evidence. Both they and Brown claimed that the voice on a tape recording, making a death threat against Brown, was Cynthia's. The recording was made at a demonstration that Cynthia had not attended. Unfortunately the barrister acting for Cynthia could have done better. The experience emphasised again to her the need for the very best and most committed legal representation for activists who might face prison.

The case was lost again, but in the 'appeal against sentence' the campaign won a small and useful victory, Cynthia was allowed to drive her car on the public roads around Hill Grove, although she was still not allowed to stop. This small freedom was to prove a real bonus.

Experience had taught Cynthia to take every opportunity to sound off. Leaving the dock and depending on the unavoidable reporter's line 'as the defendant left the dock', Cynthia shouted "British justice stinks. If I am guilty of harassment send me to prison, don't give me a silly fine."

Reflecting on her harassment case, Cynthia says now, "Yes... British justice. Phew! My whole harassment case stank from beginning to end. It was their way of stopping me protesting and denying my freedom. I took heart from the fact that it was a sign of how desperate the enemy was." She did try to get her case back before the Criminal Cases Review Commission, but despite concrete evidence that perjury had taken place, Cynthia remains "a criminal" to this day.

In September, twenty five year old Ben Thompson, serving a three month sentence after a Hill Grove farm demonstration, ended a hunger strike in Bullingdon prison, after his demands for a vegan diet free of genetically modified foods was met by the prison authorities.

Park and Demonstrate -Saturday 17ᵗʰ October

The demonstration on Saturday October 17 was in support of hunger striker Barry Horne, the Save the Hill Grove Cats campaign announced.[4] Horne had been sentenced to 18 years imprisonment for animal rights related arson attacks on premises on the Isle of Wight, with a concurrent 14-year sentence for attempted arson in Bristol. On hunger strike he demanded a 'A genuine

---

4 At the time of the demonstration, Horne was into his 42ⁿᵈ day of hunger strike in protest at the Government's failure to act on pre-election promises. Activists held a 24 hour hunger strike in sympathy with him outside the home of the Home Office Minister Jack Straw in Minster Lovell. Barry Horne, animal liberation activist and anti-racist, died on Nov 5ᵗʰ 2001 in Worcester hospital, while serving an 18 year prison sentence. His principle demand during the 68 days of his third hunger strike was that New Labour fulfil their election manifesto pledge in *New Labour New Li(f)e* to hold a Royal Comission into vivisection; a promise that they had made partially as a consequence of Barry's first hunger strike in 1997. Although a Labour MP negotiated with Barry's lawyers in the last weeks of his hunger strike, when he died New Labour went on with business as usual.

and unconditional commitment to adopt and implement policies that will bring a final end to all vivisection for whatever purposes, by a date no later than January 6th 2002.'

The campaign organisers refused to meet with Thames Valley Police, to discuss their plans for their next demonstration. The cost of policing Hill Grove now stood at £1.25M and the police were coming under considerable pressure to meet with demonstrators and get them to help police themselves.[5]

To advertise the march, activists locked themselves inside Carfax Tower in the busy shopping centre of Oxford and unfurled a banner which read "Hill Grove farm breeds cats for torture: Next Demo Sat. 17 Oct. 12PM. Show you care. Join us."

Asked about the publicity, Heather James, spokeswoman for the campaign, said: "I think it's great." She said that the protesters had similar stunts planned for the future. She told one local paper, with the confidence of a seasoned political propagandist: "As far as I'm concerned this is just the beginning. We've only just started."

The demonstrators took their cause to the centre of Oxford, creating maximum disruption to Saturday consumers. At least 1,000 protesters descended on the city centre. Reinforcements from West Mercia and Hampshire police and mounted officers from the Metropolitan force were drafted in as the scale of the demonstration took police by surprise. Buses had to be diverted around Cornmarket, causing tailbacks and, as the protesters began marching down Banbury Road, traffic on the major artery into the city centre ground to a halt. Twelve demonstrators were arrested for breach of the peace, obstructing police officers, minor public order offences, and one person for possession of a penknife.

Part of the demonstration called first at the home of Prof. Blakemore. Mounted police soon blocked off the roads but the

---

5 In fact after this demonstration in Oxford, the campaign did meet with the police in London at the offices of Liberty, but nothing was organised. *Gazette* of 28th October 1998.

demonstration was by then quite near Blakemore's house and demonstrators used the opportunity to tell him what they thought of him. Prior to the demonstration, large notices had been posted around Oxford giving the names of other local vivisectors. Here and there, police teams guarded houses.

The exclusion orders around Hill Grove farm would eventually become a millstone around the necks of the police. At this demonstration, Dr Vernon Coleman, who had travelled to Witney to address the demonstration, decided to sue the police for having ordered a *de-facto* ban on the demonstration by placing an exclusion order around the farm. In a case scheduled for December in Oxford County Court, Coleman claimed back his travel expenses, the sum of £99.80 from Thames Valley Police.

As Barry Horne's condition worsened, around the 59th day of a hunger strike, the Animal Rights Militia (ARM) appeared to step up its pressure on the Government. The *Oxford Times*[6] carried a report of alleged assassination threats against Christopher Brown and Prof. Blakemore, in the event of Horne dying. In December, two more Hill Grove activists, Thomas and Anna Monaghan from East Sussex, were sent to prison.[7]

Daniel's Experience

Once again we are all wakened by the singing blackbird that always sat in the tree above us. It was quite hard to get to sleep at Hill Grove sometimes, because of the fireworks.

We wait for the workers coming in, getting far back in the hedge in case they try and run us over. You then hear a car coming up Dry Lane, you tense yourself thinking it's a worker and you get ready to shout, only to find music blaring out, lights flashing and Cynthia shouting.

---

6 *Oxford Times* December 4, 1998.
7 *Oxford Mail* December 7, 1998.

A packet of food, sweets and nuts normally would be thrown out of the window and we would try catching them as they flew towards us, remembering she can't stop or she would be arrested.

In come the workers, out comes Christopher Brown on his tractor with one window taped up after the Battle of Hill Grove. Out comes Katherine to go to the tennis match. I shout at all of the staff and I tell them they will have to leave Hill Grove after we close it down. They don't dare tell people where they work, some of them say they work for the Blue Cross.

Also I shout that the police are evident guarding the farm. The holiday and bed and breakfast people come in and out. Some stop and ask what we are doing. I have been at Hill Grove when they have gone home crying.

I have seen some foul sights at Hill Grove. Once I saw a police officer shout at a protester so loud her ears were ringing and she had to go to hospital. I saw the police beating up an elderly woman and one person had his hands and feet handcuffed; absolutely disgusting.

I think back now, 400 people arrested, 27 imprisoned. We stop Brown and I asked him if he felt good about his cats screaming in pain. As he ignores us, I say: "What goes around comes around."

Chapter Nineteen

🐈 Cat Lobby Hits City

It opens a wide field for doing good, to men of virtue, talent and abilities, who love their country and glory in its prosperity. Such men will speedily perceive, that this prosperity can only be of short duration, if public morals are neglected...[1]

Cynthia O'Neill is an exceptionally resourceful woman and like all good rebels and radicals, she learnt quickly how to subvert the restraining orders the State brought against her. Not being allowed to be stationary in her car or on foot within a mile radius of Hill Grove farm, initially seemed like a death sentence.

Cynthia, quickly learnt to go past the demonstrations, pickets and vigils, becoming adept at throwing her contribution to the cold, tired protesters out of the car window. She also choreographed a "traffic light ballet," with legal reason to stop on the road for short periods. Being careful to keep up with the traffic, level with the protesters, she would open both windows and let out a full blast of rousing music. The Dam Busters March, she recalls was popular, The Grenadiers most appropriate and Old Brown's Body delightful and cheering. After six returns to the lights with police becoming more and more angry, she had to be satisfied with her work.

---

1 Patrick Colquhoun, *A Treatise on the Police of the Metropolis; containing a detail of the various crimes and misdemeanors by which public and private property and security are, at present, injured and endangered: and suggesting remedies for their prevention*. Fifth edition, London 1797.

On one occasion when Cynthia was performing, two well known TVP officers, Petit & Lay, gave chase. She says: "...all the usual ensued. I was not breaking the injunction in any way. They said, I was breaking "the spirit of the injunction." "Oh, Yes", I responded, "Cats don't have souls but injunctions do!" "The injunction said I must not stop my car within the one-mile danger zone and stop it I did not. The red traffic lights were not under my control."

Park and Demonstrate
-Saturday December 12 1998

The December demonstration headed straight for Oxford City centre with the intention of disrupting Christmas consumerism. In the local papers, after the demonstration much of the discussion placed commerce and animal rights in stark contradiction. The *Witney Gazette* plucked an unattributed half a million pounds in lost sales from thin air.[2] The *Gazette* quoted Mr Marcus Lapthorn, apparently the 'manager' of Oxford City centre, "It was a very frightening situation for the public and brought public transport to a halt. It has done a lot of damage to Oxford as a safe place to shop." Mr Lapthorn had nothing to say about *Oxford as a safe place* for citizens to become actively involved in democracy.

In not directly blaming the police for the chaos, the city centre 'manager' and others were letting prejudice get in the way of rationality. As a Save the Hill Grove Cats spokesman said following the protest: "The serious monetary loss to shops in Oxford City centre is directly linked to the banning of the demonstrations (around the farm). Just what is going on when the police are happier to see demonstrators in a busy city centre than at isolated Hill Grove farm?"

Many local Witney people were later to complain that the police had set up roadblocks and searched cars and their occupants. One resident, expecting the chimney sweep was angry

---

2 *Witney Gazette* December 16, 1998.

when he failed to arrive: "I was waiting for the chimney sweep on Saturday morning. Half an hour after he was due to arrive I received a telephone call from him saying that he had tried three different routes to enter Witney but had been unable to do so because police had stopped him. This despite the fact that, dirty from his work, the sweep had shown the police his brushes stowed in the rear of the van. However, a minibus full of masked demonstrators in combat gear was able to park close to my home shortly after."[3] This particular complainant like many others blamed the demonstrators for demonstrating, rather than the police for curtailing democratic rights.

During the demonstration's ragged track through Oxford centre, twenty-six people were arrested for public order offences. However, as in many such circumstances, who actually created the public disorder was an open question in the minds of some observers. *Thames Valley FM*, a local radio station had two reporters in Oxford City centre. At midday one of them commented: "The demonstration is quite violent. However, I have to say that most of the violence is coming from the police."

'Ashamed' of Oxford had a letter published in the *Oxford Mail* of December 21. She was, she said, writing with reference to the animal rights protest march, which took place in Oxford City centre on Saturday, December 12th:

I was not a part of the march. I was in the City centre shopping and happened to walk past the area in which it was taking place. I stood and watched the protesters and police for about an hour with my mother, who was also with me.

I would like to draw your attention to a totally unbiased outsider's view of the events of that day.

I was shocked to say the least to see the way that the police treated the protesters. In particular, I witnessed the police forcing people to move by pushing against them with their horses. I

3 *The Witney Gazette* December 16, 1998.

could hear people screaming as they were pressed against a wall and crushed by their fellow protesters as the police increased the pressure.

These people in question were elderly people, children and people in wheelchairs. Hardly a threat to the police and definitely not in any way antagonising the police. I was further amazed to see one policewoman raise her baton above her head and bring it down into this crowd. There were between 50 and 100 people watching this alongside me and I did not hear one person say the police were justified in their actions. My mother actually made the comment that she was ashamed of the police, and I must agree with that sentiment.

I am fairly confident that you will not print this letter, but maybe you could bear it in mind when you next report on one of these marches.

Bed and Barrier

In December, the Advertising Standards Authority (ASA) gave a ruling on Mr. Brown's bed and breakfast enterprise, which Cynthia O'Neill had reported some years before.[4] The Authority finally demanded that Brown stopped describing the B&B business as "friendly". Even the ASA realised that with a sporadic demonstration of thousands, only stopped from sacking the farm by a constantly re-issued five mile exclusion order and a virtual metal wall around the farm, the atmosphere for the B&B could now hardly be described as "friendly".

In December both national and local papers reported a steady build up of parliamentary pressure in support of the campaign.[5, 6] A Common's motion backed by almost 50 Labour and Lib-Dem MPs and due to be heard in the New Year, demanded that the Home Secretary, Jack Straw, outlawed the practice of sending cats abroad to be used by vivisectors. Export of animals

---

4 *Oxford Mail* December 23, 1998.
5 *The Daily Express* December 12, 1998.
6 *Oxford Mail* December 22, 1998.

for vivisection was legal under the 1986 Animals (Scientific Procedures) Act and the motion, due to be tabled by Labour MP Lawrence Cunliffe, called for the law to be changed.

As well as a change in the law, Lawrence Cunlife wanted an investigation into Hill Grove farm and its procedures. Jack Straw, however, tied by New Labour's attachment to the pharmaceutical companies and genetic engineering industry, had no time for any alternative view of vivisection. A spokesman for Straw said: "The farm is not breaking the law. It acts as a breeding establishment under the 1986 Act, which puts in place a rigorous system of controls and stringent safeguards on animal pain and suffering."

On Christmas Day a small group of protesters carried out a demonstration, to find that Thames Valley Police provided 200 officers to control it. Was that time and a half or double time?

Telling Tales

Many people have been shocked at the length of sentences handed out to Hill Grove protesters who have fallen foul of the law. Considering the number of murderers and rapists who are back outside in months, the sentences given out for Hill Grove offences have been astonishing. Despite this, I feel it is my duty to inform on several more individuals who have shown contempt for the law. For this service, I ask only that I am paid from the Informants Fund monies which will go to the anti-vivisection cause and also that I am granted immunity.

First, for incitement to commit criminal damage, I would like to grass up the Staff of the Swindon Home Office. They have refused to answer letters, discuss the matter of Hill Grove or look into the serious, well-supported allegations at the farm. They have even refused to accept a 100,000 name petition. Given that a judge said this office should be consulted by those concerned about

Hill Grove and quoted such chats as an alternative to illegal activity, the Home Office evasiveness is sheer incitement. Now that I have given information on them, I expect that due process will immediately take its course.

I also wish to provide information against the police for harassment, assault, abusive behaviour, conduct likely to cause a breach of the peace and, following their widespread arrest of innocent protesters, false imprisonment. Having provided this information, I expect one half of the force to arrest the other half and demand that the arrested half be dealt with in a proper manner by the courts. I hold myself in readiness as a witness at this trial.

Next I have vital information against unnamed secret 'others' for breaches of the 1986 Animals (Scientific Procedures) Act relating to housing and care of animals and the 1911 Cruelty to Animal Act.

If my knowledge of the law, gleaned mainly from TV, is accurate, I expect that the provision of these informations will stand me in good stead in any future proceedings for any crime, or suspected offence I might commit. As so far I have not been charged with any offence I expect to be issued with a voucher by the Home Office, enabling me to commit any number of offences in the cause of anti-vivisection.

I wish also to take this opportunity of any amnesty offered me, to confess to offences that have not come to the attention of the law. According to current legislation, animal experiments shall not be done unless they are necessary. Through payment of taxes, however, I have helped fund thousands such experiments used by the pharmaceutical companies to determine whether drugs are suitable for human beings –all of no practical use and therefore all unnecessary. I hereby confess to this crime, prior to the receipt of my voucher.

If by some odd happenstance, the Home Office choose to penalise rather than reward me for my information, I make only one plea that I am not sent to prison with either any unnamed 'others', Home Office staff or half the police force.

Christopher Clarke

Chapter Twenty

🐈 Going Away

I was remitted to Portland Prison in February 1881. Shortly afterwards, a young blackbird came into my possession. For some months I relieved the tedium of my solitude by efforts to win the confidence of my companion. He would stand upon my breast as I lay in bed in the morning and awaken me from sleep. He would perch on the edge of my table and share my porridge.[1]

Rose, who had been arrested and left trussed on the ground during the Battle of Hill Grove, had been before the Magistrates in October for a preliminary hearing. Trying to ensure that she tendered the right plea, the police held her in the court cells for two hours and in order to give the magistrates the right impression, she was led from the cells to face the court with very tight handcuffs to both her wrists and a further handcuff locked to a security officer. Her trial date was fixed for the 5th of January 2000.

A newspaper published Brown's story on the day of Rose's trial; Would the jury be influenced by this? The judge clearly thought so for after finding that a number of them had read the article he discharged the jury. Another jury was sworn in.

Rose's trial disclosed a number of things. For instance that police cadets appeared to have started the stone throwing on the 18th April 1998. These "witnesses" were brought into court unseen and gave evidence from behind a screen -British justice, the

---

1 Michael Davitt. *Leaves from a Prison Diary,* Chapman and Hall. London. 1885.

envy of the free world! The arguments in Rose's trial revolved around complicity and incitement with frequent mention of agents provocateur. Rose was found guilty and sent to prison.

Rose, A day in the life

On February 15th 1999, I found myself unexpectedly being taken to HMP Eastwood Park Women's Prison in Gloucestershire. It was a bright, sunny but cold day. I had declined a lift from a friend to the Magistrates Court from Witney town centre thinking it would be nice to get some fresh air before my final hearing.

Aged 33, and a final year student of Environmental Science, I am one of about 18 people who went to prison for their belief that people should not be trading in the lives of sentient beings. In years to come, I hope that anyone reading this short piece will shake their heads in disgust, if not disbelief, that we allowed the abomination of vivisection to carry on unhindered in our midst for so long.

My journey to prison began at Bicester Magistrates Court. The indignity of being tightly handcuffed and then 'double cuffed' to a security guard was trivial compared to the indignity of having all my clothing removed once I arrived at prison reception. Standing in the midst of strangers with no clothing on is an experience that will always be ingrained in my memory.

Having never been in prison before, it was terrifying not knowing what lay ahead as I carried my belongings to a cell in a large, prison issue plastic bag. A female prison officer sympathetic to my predicament accompanied me. She told me she would help me to settle in. She told me that I would have to spend my time in prison in the remand wing, which is very noisy, untidy, and harbours lots of drug addicts.

The heavy metal door locked behind me with a bang, and for the first time in my life, I could not leave a room, because the key was attached to the officer's belt. "Hello new girl?" a voice called from across the corridor.

I decided to keep quiet, taking the advice of the prison officers on arrival. "Suit yourself", she replied, when no response came. I looked around me; there was a silver coloured galvanised toilet and washbasin in the corner beneath the window. The window had vertical bars covered with chipped paintwork. There was no mirror. I would not see my reflection for another 10 days; mirrors are a rarity in prisons, as they tend to get broken so easily. I could see out to a clear, starry sky, and also hear loud conversations between inmates across the courtyard.

I tried to settle in as best I could; had I been suicidal, it would have been easy to end it all then, the staff returned my coat which contained a strong belt. However, I knew that my nightmare would be just 12 days long, unlike the animals in vivisection laboratories that may spend years imprisoned before being tortured and killed. I was there precisely because of the injustices meted out to animals every hour of the day; Why would I want to die when animals have few enough friends?

It was a sleepless night, not unexpectedly, given that I had not expected to be in prison. During the night, a prisoner was taken away by staff, apparently she was a heroin addict who suffered an asthma attack. Other prisoners tried to get news of her, but the prison officers did not want to talk to them.

At eight o'clock in the morning, my door was swung open. "Breakfast?" I was asked by a cheerful man with a Bristol accent. "Why not?" I ask and walked out of the cell for the first time in 12 hours. Walking along the corridor as the "new girl" I found myself being stared at and then pushed to the back of the queue to leave the wing. Not looking for trouble, I accept this.

On the evening of my arrival at prison an inmate warned me that I could "expect trouble from the staff" because I had been convicted of assaulting a "fellow uniform." It is another uncertainty to add to those which are already swirling around in my head.

After breakfast, which consisted of a cup of soya milk, cereal and dry toast, I am told to expect a meeting with the governor, who will ask me questions about my conviction and the "standards of behaviour expected of me during my time in prison." An officer took me through several locked gates. Being unable to open a door and walk through without having to stop, is a situation I became used to over the next 12 days. Standing in a stark waiting room, I noticed ominously that the chairs were bolted to the floor. Outside raised voices echoed in the corridor, looking through the window, I strained to see the commotion.

Two male officers were expertly subduing a heavily built young woman with bleached hair, leading her along the corridor with her head pushed towards her chest. She was trying to stand upright, but was forced to walk in a crouched position, unable to see where she was going. "I didn't start it Sir," she protested loudly as she was forced along. I later found that the woman spent eighteen days in solitary confinement for causing a riot in the dining room. The number of male prison officers here take a lot of new prisoners by surprise. I had expected an all female cast. My thoughts were interrupted by a woman's voice. "Come in," she said almost cheerfully.

A tall man in a pristine white shirt and black trousers stood behind a large desk. Around 40 years old, with dark hair and dark brown eyes, his expression is not as unfriendly as I had expected. The conversation with the inmate who had said I could expect trouble from the officers for being convicted of threatening behaviour to the

police may not be quite right. I tried not to be too com-
placent about the fact that he seemed somehow compassionate, if not sympathetic to me.

"Sit down sweetheart", he said calmly, gesturing me to
a seat next to the female officer.

"Thank you," I replied, taking the seat.

"You got a new tracksuit last night," he smiled.

It took a few seconds to overcome my shock at being
smiled at.

"I am so tall, they had to go to the store for some new
clothes, so it is a privilege," I said, relaxing slightly.

Opening the folder in front of him, the Governor
glanced at the first few pages.

"No drugs, not a smoker, vegan! I think you must be
the healthiest prisoner we have had for some time," he
declared, smiling broadly.

Flattered by this unexpectedly kind treatment, it was
difficult to take seriously the conversation with that inmate the previous evening.

"Do you know why you are here?" he asked.

"Because I showed compassion for those with no
voice," I reply.

"You are here because you showed threatening
behaviour to police officers at Hill Grove farm," he replied.

"If you say so, sir," I replied, knowing that the police
at Hill Grove were wearing full riot gear on the day the
supposed offence was committed. My only potential wea-
pon had been an asthma inhaler.

"Are you going to accept this sentence and help us to
help you?" he asked.

"I will help you to help me, but I will never accept a sentence for showing concern to animals. I make no apology for my love of them."

"You are a student of environmental science?" he paused, looking at the file again.

"A smart girl. I would use that intelligence to get through the time you spend here. You are different to the norm in this place, some people don't like intelligence, but I am sure you will keep your head down. You don't look the type to smack a copper," he finished.

"I didn't smack a copper," I protested.

"They all deny why they are in here, I expect you're no different," he responded.

"You can go," he said, as the female officer got ready to escort me out.

I was not allowed to walk unaccompanied and another female officer escorted me back to the wing. I was becoming accustomed to the smell of disinfectant, rattling doors, keys jangling, and the prison clothing worn by various groups. Brightly coloured trousers, and shirts for those employed outdoors, and white clothing for catering staff.

"Can I apply for a job?" I asked my companion.

"I don't think you'll be here long enough to apply. I am sure that you could work outdoors, being that way inclined," she smiled.

It surprised me how much information these people have about my background, especially as I had only arrived last night.

Back at the cell, the officer who accompanied me asked me to wait at the cell door. She went but returned a while later with a letter from my solicitor, before I could take it from her hand she tore the envelope for me. "Solicitors rule," she said and it was clear to me that mail was opened and read before being delivered to prisoners. Locked in my cell once more, it was quiet enough to sit on the bed to read the letter without interruptions. A legal visit had been booked for the following week and the solicitor's staff offered their support.

About an hour later, a male officer opened the hatch on the cell door, looked into the cell and asked me to "make myself decent" to go to the doctor. Feeling fine, I declined his request. "You have to go love, you must be seen by the doctor even if you feel alright," he persisted; finally he opened the door and came into the cell.

"They took my inhalers, Sir, so I have no reason to go," I say standing up to face him.

"Rules are rules, so come on" he said, as he glanced at his watch.

"They will order more, it will take about a week. Orders are to bring you, so let's have you outside now," he said a little more sternly.

Getting used to walking accompanied at all times, I waited to stand at three different sets of locked gates, while he let me through each time.

"Are you the animal rights lady?" he asked.

"Yes," I replied calmly, feeling in no mood for conversation.

"Is it true you smacked a copper?" he enquired, looking down at me as we walked.

"No, it's not true. Do you think I am capable of that? The plea was not guilty since my arrest 10 months ago; there is nothing that I need to apologise for" was my curt reply.

"All the women here deny the reasons why they were sent, but if it is any consolation to you, you won't get any problems from me; cruelty to animals sickens me just as much," he said and smiled sympathetically.

The officer knocked on the door of the surgery, beckoning me in from the corridor where I had been waiting.

The doctor's surgery was small, clean and smelled of disinfectant. A female nurse sat near the medicine trolley. The doctor sat behind a small desk covered in papers and files. Beckoning me to sit down, he opened a file on his desk.

"Are you alright?" he probed.

"What about my inhalers Doctor, what can I do if anything happens in the night?" I replied.

"They will take about a week, in the meantime you can use Ventolin."

"Ventolin gives me tremors and a rapid heartbeat, my own doctor refuses to prescribe it. Is there anything else?" I reply, as I began to feel somewhat panicky in case an attack came.

"Can my friend send my homoeopathic medicine in here?" I asked, beginning to feel stressed.

He shruged his shoulders inarticulately and continued to write notes on the file.

"Is that it?" I wonder, surprised that he didn't want to help.

He nodded, without lifting his eyes from the papers in front of him.

Banging the door on the way out, I felt very angry that a doctor could be so uncaring. The officer who had waited, ordered me to slow down, as we walked along the corridor, he couldn't keep up with me!

"Calm down love, what is it?" he asked, surprised at my rush to get away from the room.

"They won't give me temporary medication, what kind of place is this?" I asked, almost in tears.

We walked back to my wing in silence once more, as he opened the door of the cell and I thanked him for listening to me. The door banged shut and I sat on the bed until called for lunch. Lunch consisted of thick vegetable soup, bread and an apple. The governors had decided to give me an extra cup of soya milk with each meal. Some of the other inmates asked if I was pregnant because there was extra milk available to me; at least I did not have that complication to deal with.

A blond woman about my age, walked up and asks 'Hill Grove?' I look at her, and she offers her hand to shake mine. She tells me that she had come to prison the previous week. I offered her a seat, not believing my luck that there is another person in this awful place who has been convicted of an offence relating to Hill Grove farm. Suddenly, the feelings of isolation and fear lessened as we sat for the short time before being called back to the wing. She said she would see me for education classes and gym training; it turned out that she was in the wing above mine, so we could meet at dinner times.

We did meet and how thankful I was to my new friend who helped me get through those awful days until my longed for release.

Rose

Chapter Twenty One

🐈 An Eye for Business

"You the jury", an Oxford Courier column, asked readers: "Do you think the cat breeding farm should be shut down?" 95% of those who answered voted in favour.

While Rose was locked away, others kept watch and thanks to expert observation, skilled driving and determination, some campaigners followed Brown on one of his visits, his white van full of "stock". It was a long ride, to the notorious Huntingdon Life Sciences labs in Cambridgeshire. What would be done to these kittens? What terrible experiments would they be subjected to?

The campaign was definitely getting to Brown. In January, 1999, he made an offer to sell the Hill Grove cats to the campaign for £200,000.[1] The campaign immediately turned the offer to its advantage, prosaically terming the price "blood money."

The campaign took a clear stand on the offer, immediately capturing the moral high ground. Greg Jennings put it well, saying that the campaign would not "give in to *blackmail*," and accused Mr Brown of using *hostage tactics*. In fact, time and again the campaign outflanked Brown, the police and opposition commentators when it came to public relations. Jennings went on: "I don't think any protester would feel comfortable giving money to Mr Brown… we don't believe that farmer Brown should be rewarded for what he has been doing. This offer is a sign that he

---

1 *Oxford Mail* January 8, 1999.

is not operating from a position of strength and is weakening. He has clearly had enough and simply wants a way out without losing face."[2] Jennings called on Brown to shut down his farm and turn over the cats to the Cats Protection League.

Apart from harassing protesters the police also clobbered reporters! In decidedly poor public relations moves, in February Nick Cobbing of the German *Stern* and Roddy Mansfield of the Oxford based *Undercurrents Productions* were both given the full works, complete with Thames Valley police handcuffs and arm-locks!

On the 1st Feb 1999, another petition of 150,000 signatures was handed in to the Home Office. The total number of signatures now handed over came to 350,000. Every one was ignored. Still trying proper channels!

Despite a very cold February, 1,500 people attended that next demonstration and fortunately the sun shone. The local Witney Football Club, having a match booked for the same day as the march, became sour on learning of the demonstration. Cynthia, able to reflect humorously on anything, joked that as the attendance at the demonstration would be far higher than that at the football match, the footballers and their supporters would be better joining the march!

By now, the possible price for participating in democracy was clear to the protesters. The previous week, Judge King had sent seven more anti-vivisectors to prison, they and most others had no previous convictions, not even motoring offences; the Battle was hotting up. The defendants Suzanne Amos, Peter Merson-Davies, Timothy Senior, Paul Holliday, David Lakeman, Lucy Richards and Wendy Nicolaou all pleaded guilty to offences of violent disorder committed the previous April, and received more than five years in jail between them, with individual sentences ranging from eight months to a year.[3]

---

2 Ibid.
3 *Oxford Times* February 19, 1999.

During the mass trespass, the prosecution said: "Missiles, including rocks and stones were thrown at the farm house, causing considerable damage." A total of 60 windows and roof tiles worth £3,000 were broken and police were at risk of injury."

Realising that the exclusion order had made a rod for their own backs, the police allowed –despite it being their basic right to protest– demonstrators back at Hill Grove farm. Over 1,000 protesters converged on Witney on a Saturday to march to Hill Grove farm. The agreement, to be able to stay for one hour immediately outside the farm, was the result of talks carried out between the police and the campaign. Not only had the exclusion order led to demonstrators pouring into Oxford and Witney, disrupting commercial relations, but everything which the police did had been observed by independent onlookers.

Speeches were held at Witney Recreation Ground and then the demonstrators walked to Hill Grove farm where two children laid flowers at the end of Brown's driveway. In defiance of the agreement arrived at between the campaign and the police, about 250 protesters strayed into the fields surrounding the farm. According to the police later, these demonstrators were given an hour and a half to move back, after this time, the police cleared the fields using horses.

Thirty five year old Debbie Hillier travelled from Cambridge with her twelve year old daughter to attend the protest near Minster Lovell. She was knocked to the ground by a mounted officer, who was alleged to have swung his horse around and ridden over her. She was taken to John Radcliffe Hospital in Oxford with a broken ankle and campaigners claim she had a hoof print on her upper thigh and possible damaged kidneys.[4]

After an operation on her ankle, Debbie decided that she wanted to talk to the media, and suddenly the hospital became a prison. One journalist who managed to speak to her on the phone wanted to carry out an interview. As the journalist approached

---

4 *The Standard* February 25, 1999.

Debbie's ward with Greg Jennings, three security guards grabbed them and threw the two men out. The Press Officer from the John Radcliffe, told the reporter that it wasn't Debbie he had spoken to but someone from the campaign and actually Debbie did not want to see anyone!

Debbie's ward became a fortress, no one except her husband could visit, and even he had difficulty! Debbie couldn't make any calls out and no calls were put through to her. If anyone rang the hospital and asked for Debbie the phone would be hung up. How incredible that a Trust should collude with the police in this way!

Around this time, Witney police found themselves carrying out an investigation after a telegraph pole carrying phone lines to Hill Grove farm was cut down. The pole on the edge of Dry Lane was sawn through at 2.30am one Monday morning.

Both Cynthia and the broader campaign came to understand the benefit to them in ensuring that the police turned out for the smallest demonstration; not only did it make the police look as if they were being heavy handed, they were burning up financial resources. In her diary, Cynthia wrote: "Every demo counted, even when only two people or even one were present, it was something that needed a Thames Valley police escort! Every Sunday despite the cold and the wet protests continued."

An observant protester, visiting the Parish Church used by the Brown family and the Home Office Minister, noticed that none other than Jack Straw would soon be reading the Lesson. Was this a public show of commitment to Brown by the government? On a cold evening several protesters arrived outside the church to deliver a more than polite 'Happy Easter', to be greeted in return by scowls and heads hung low in shame. *The Express*[5] reported: "Straw has kittens as 'Save the Cats' protesters gather outside church," showing a photo of the Minister leaving church.

5 *Daily Express* April 5, 1999.

Chapter Twenty Two

🐈 Lab Animals Day

Vivisection is scientific and medical fraud. Next time you are ill farmer Brown, go and see a vet.[1]

Policing costs were reported to be around £2M at the time of the Lab Animals Day demonstration on 17th April 1999. The campaign suggested that this was a low estimate. Often working round the clock, campaigners organised intently for the demonstration. Adverts placed in the *Big Issue* brought many new faces and activists from Europe pledged their support.

Two German supporters who Cynthia had been corresponding with, Dagmar and Roswitha who had previously sent a cheque for £891 from German friends, arrived in England for the April demonstration with another 20,000 signatures to add to the Hill Grove petition.

Cynthia found it so hard not being part of the demonstration. In the morning she put up posters with Dagmar and Roswitha and then went to sit on the boundary line watching the cars and coaches arriving and observing the police gathering. As the helicopter came nearer indicating that the march was on its way, Cynthia got ready. The massive, roaring, jubilant yet tired crowd, young and old, babies and pensioners, all united as they passed her roaring "Close down farmer Brown!", to which she added through the megaphone: "The quicker the better."

---

1 One of Cynthia's slogans.

Yet another march through Witney drove some local residents to fury. The local papers seemed to enjoy Witney residents blowing hot air and purple copy. However, the letters against the campaign were often so inarticulate that the campaign must have been eternally grateful that none of the writers were cat lovers.

Mr Ken Smith, of Witney, told the *Gazette*: "I've lived in Witney all my life and I'm fed up with these people coming here. It's about time they cleared off. They are coming from all over the place, even Germany, and I don't think they should be taking over our town."[2]

Mr Davis Ireson, who also lived in Witney, said: "I feel it's like rent a mob. People here have to earn a living and they are stopping people coming into town. I can understand businesses who pay rates getting angry about it."[3]

Another Witney resident, Miss Edda Bone, said: "The demos are hitting ordinary people. We were in the street when a demo came through and the police on horseback told us to go inside a pub out of the way and not come out. That's not right."[4]

Mr Wilfred Dix told the *Gazette*: "The demonstrators should be made to pay for the policing, it's getting out of hand. The man's got a licence to breed cats".[5]

In a letter headed *No Discipline,* an anonymous writer expressed the traditional authoritarian view levelled at any kind of participatory democracy.

My personal view is that most demonstrators are just a bunch of Social Security funded troublemakers hell bent on disrupting society. We have seen it all before at the likes of Greenham Common, etc. If they really wanted to support cats then surely the best thing would be to buy out farmer Brown as mentioned

---

2 *The Gazette* April 28, 1999.
3 Ibid.
4 Ibid.
5 *Witney Gazette* April 28, 1999.

before. Instead of giving money to this idea they just want to spend their money travelling to and partaking in useless demonstrations that benefit no one.[6]

A Mr Woollard of Witney expressed similar views but added an intriguing question about balaclava's.

Firstly, 1,300 demonstrators do not come from Witney. Given that coaches are used to ferry these people about, where is the money coming from to pay their expenses? I would suspect either privately or by state benefit obtained by these people. Secondly, why do these people go to public houses on Church Green and drink beer full faced then find the need to don balaclavas and helmets when leaving to attend a peaceful demonstration? These demonstrators are against cruelty to animals but the protesters do not object to striking police officers who they happily refer to as "pigs". Peaceful demonstrations, my foot! If you say political activists you are getting closer to the truth.[7]

Intimidation

A demonstration on the 15th May 1999 followed the last one in April and I went to Witney to join it. This was my second visit to Hill Grove, and I was prepared to accept the regulations attached to a gathering of this kind, which are set out in the paper "Imposing conditions on a Public Assembly", which was handed out by the police.

What I was not prepared for was being threatened with immediate arrest when I asked for permission to leave the procession for a few moments to visit a public lavatory; not being allowed to pause in a march for long enough to scrape dog dirt off my shoes, being ordered to "walk faster", and worst of all, being forced on by police orders, risking the hooves of a nervous, over-excited horse that was kicking out behind.

---

6 *Witney Gazette* May 5, 1999.
7 Ibid.

Overall, police presence at the demonstration was overwhelming, particularly in view of the small number of demonstrators. Even more sinister, there was an invisible cordon around the town of Witney. Under police orders, the coach I travelled down in (which was privately booked for supporters of the campaign) was not allowed to stop at services within a certain radius, which meant that for the duration of the event, no one was allowed access to the toilets, or refreshments, other than those they had brought with them. With five hours at Hill Grove and about 45 minutes each way on the outskirts of the town, for nearly seven hours, everyone who attended this demonstration was forced to sacrifice their basic human rights to be comfortable, and to be free of harassment and danger.

Overall, I was shocked and appalled that people who had done nothing wrong could be treated like this by our police force. When exercising your right to peaceful protest means that you'll get arrested, you really have no rights at all.

On the earlier visit, when we pulled in at the coach park, police officers strode along the side of the coach thumping the bodywork and staring in with expressionless faces. That made me feel as though I was being herded in some kind of prison convoy under an oppressive regime, dehumanised, intimidated and despised for doing no more than exercising my right to peaceful protest.

I wrote to my MP, Fabian Hamilton, about all this asking certain questions about the funding of this massive exercise in human rights abuses. My first letter was lost, subsequent letters not acknowledged officially but, through a friend, Fabian passed the message that he would get to work on the problem and contact me. Nine and a half months after my enquiry, I was still waiting.

Sue Murray

There were scenes of jubilation in Oxford Crown Court on the 28th May as three protesters, Colin Stewart, Reginald Auton and Kathryn Lawrence, all narrowly escaped jail sentences. Recorder Guy Hungerford opted to sentence all three to 200 hours community service, while handing out fines to the value of £996 and levying £200 on each defendant towards costs.

In comparison with the mainly letters from those who opposed the Hill Grove demonstration, letters to the local press from supporters were articulate and concise. Throughout the campaign there was a moral and political hegemony which unified the protesters.

Hill Grove Farm

I read with dismay and sadness the disturbing letter from R. Thomson regarding the demonstrations at Hill Grove farm. Thomson is obviously unaware of a number of things.

A recent Mori poll regarding vivisection showed that the vast majority of British people do not support the use of live animals in experiments. There are many modern methods of medical or product safety testing which do not involve using animals. I urge Thomson to read material from the Lord Downing Fund[8] or any other research centre which carry out cruelty free research.

The reason the government still allows live animal experiments is because the laboratories which test on animals are shrouded in secrecy, in order to keep information regarding the experiments carried out on three million animals a year, from us, the general public. The information, if it were made more readily available, would no doubt lead to a public outcry.

For the past two years, I have been campaigning against vivisection, and this has involved attending campaigns at Hill Grove. Perhaps Thomson would like to come with me on the next demonstration on June 12th, so that he/she can see that we are not a bunch of "dazed and distressed women manoeuvred by Animal Rights activists!" And that we are a compassionate group of people concerned with animal and human welfare who carry on a campaign which has been running for over 100 years, against all animals cruelly tested on, not just cats!

The language of Thomson's letter was one of a selfish individual who cares only for his own "cabbage patch"! I would like him to know that if they were in a cage, with an electrode stuck in their head, we would be doing all we could to release them back to freedom.

Miss H.M. Large BSc (Hons), MSc.MRAC-Fairford.[8]

Plain Arguments Against Vivisection

The breeding of cats at Hill Grove farm for vivisection is legal and sanctioned by the government and as far as R. Thomson is concerned (letters 27th May) that is that. Of course, left to the individuals like R. Thomson, we would no doubt still be burning people at the stake and sending small children to work in the mines.

The belief that medical advances now available to our children have been enhanced by tests done on animals is belied by the staggering increases in childhood diseases like asthma, diabetes and obesity, levels which are only surpassed by those in America.

Yes, it's true that cats kill creatures smaller than themselves, but then, so do we. We truck them thousands of miles around Europe, chase them across the countryside on horseback, shoot them out of the sky, imprison them in cages and pens that are too small, drag them out of rivers with a hook and mutilate them in laboratories.

However, cruel as all these things are, they are legal, so R. Thomson can carry on gardening with an untroubled conscience. In fact, we know from the final paragraph of Thomson's letter that what really stirs the ire in the shires is the cat poo in the border!

V.A. Kneebone. Easton in Gordano.[9]

---

8 *Standard* of June 3rd 1999.
9 Ibid.

Well attended demonstrations now took place all day Saturday and vigils were until the Sunday, day shift took over, sending the Browns a constant message loud and clear "No surrender."

In the background, militants continued to carry out a kind of low level military harassment of rescue raids on the farm, letting Brown, the police and the vivisectionists know that the campaigners were still utterly committed.

The local papers had problems dealing with the many letters which they received and consequently their publication was spread over weeks during which time, they lost their immediate news value. This letter was published almost a month after the June demonstration to which it alludes.

Uniformed Bullies

Thames Valley police actions at Hill Grove farm demonstrations finally hit an all time low on Saturday 12th June, with an extremely ugly incident in Oxford when a pregnant woman was punched in the stomach by a Thames Valley police officer.

I would appeal to local councillors, the media and the general public to start asking some very serious questions about the style and attitude of policing they want to see in this area.

Are we going to put up with this sort of undisciplined and dangerous violent conduct from our local police force? I think that we deserve a better quality of policing than one which stoops to these depths.

Make Thames Valley police account for their actions. Make them become more disciplined and not a law unto themselves.

We want law and order administered in a fair manner for everyone, not by means of violent assaults by bullies in uniform.

K. B. Witney.[10]

---

10 *Witney Gazette* July 7, 1999.

Chapter Twenty Three

 **A Whiff of Defeat**

Freedom only to speak inoffensively is not worth having.[1]

After a July night vigil, a number of the protesters found that they were ill and it was suspected that organophosphate pesticide had again been sprayed on the verges approaching the farm. Cynthia told the *Oxford Mail*[2] about one of the youngest protesters. "I have been told a 12 year old lad from Cirencester, who joins us on a regular basis, has been complaining of a sore throat, feeling sick and a general malaise."

The campaign also complained again to West Oxfordshire District Council, only to be told that they did not have the money to investigate.[3] The Director of Environmental Services denied refusing to investigate saying: "Allegation that West Oxfordshire District Council is refusing to investigate this matter due to lack of available funds is totally inaccurate. The issue that is being described is an allegation of improper use of pesticides, which is controlled under the Food and Environmental Protection Act. The enforcing authority is the Health and Safety Executive and we will forward the matter to them."[4]

---

1 Judge Taylor quoting a Court of Appeal judgement in the succesful appeal of Andrew Kirk in September 2000. Kirk was originally arrested after protesting outside a Middlesbrough bank on behalf of the Hill Grove cats, with a "bloodstained white coat" and pictures of vivisected animals.
2 *Oxford Mail* July 6, 1999.
3 Ibid.
4 *Oxford Mail* July 6, 1999.

The Last Demonstration

On Saturday 31st July 1999, the campaigners marched through Witney town centre. This demonstration, the previous one through Witney and the one through the centre of Oxford, fanned the flames of the cause well beyond the patch of mud outside the farm that had witnessed protests over the last eight years. As a consequence of these two demonstrations, local and some national papers were full of a debate which raged between the quiet and conventional residents of these typically English towns and villages, and the equally English and for all one knows equally conventional animal lovers of the campaign.

Cynthia O'Neill at this time was under order of the court not allowed to stop her car anywhere within a radius of the farm, the Oxford University Laboratories or the house of Colin Blakemore. To make matters worse, she now found that the police had 24 hours surveillance of her.[5]

Cynthia was now a figure-head unable to participate in any of the protests, demonstrations or actions. She was left to observe, she had been strategically excluded from the struggle. Others had taken up the baton, the campaign had attracted large numbers of capable people, it now had an office, staff and a regular newsletter. In the style of many other "life style" demonstrations since the 1980s it had attracted people who knew perhaps for the first time in their lives, that this was something they had to do. Volunteers had come forward who had made clear decisions to put this campaign the centre of their lives.

---

5 Cynthia found out about the surveillance after speaking to an amateur radio enthusiast who had been listening to police messages which reported Cynthia's movements in detail, right down to the time at which her bedroom light went off for the night and when she attended hospital. It was clear the police who observed her wanted to catch her breaking the injunction imposed upon her.

A drop in the ocean

My involvement with the campaign to close Hill Grove farm was a drop in the ocean compared with most. My story starts in late May of 1999 when, entering the office of my local animal rescue centre, my attention was seized by a small poster headed "Born to Die."

There I saw a large ginger cat, its back, side and front shaved, it was laying on two sheets of thick plastic with two leather straps, one around its neck and the other around its middle, joined by a third much stiffer strap holding the first two apart. It had this appalling blue foam bubbling out of its head, and so many plastic tubes and caps, some with blood in them, that I couldn't count them.

This dear cat had its tail so far under it that it was touching its forelegs, but the vilest, most horrendous thing was that this cat still appeared to be alive. It was time for me to become active. On my first outing, however, I didn't ever get to Hill Grove farm; I was arrested in Witney before the demonstration moved off.

As the protesters marched out towards the farm, I was being frog marched by the police to the awaiting prison van and was locked in a cage. I hated it; apart from being extremely hot, it was claustrophobic, and I was scared! Then suddenly a thought came to me. I am imprisoned for a while and I am going to get out, I knew that. I can comprehend, I can understand and I can reason. But what about the tormented minds of those Hill Grove cats. I still didn't like it, but I could look beyond my own fears.

Rae Newbold

Following the July demonstration, Witney and its residents teetered on the brink of civil war, the local papers were inundated with mail for and against the demonstrators and the Editor of the *Gazette* decided to nail his colours to the mast in no uncertain manner. On August 4th, the *Gazette*'s front page carried a page length photograph with the slogan That's Enough. The editorial made for sobering reading; it epitomised the voice of commerce and the middle classes who considered any serious discussion of ethics, animal rights or vivisection as a divergence from the true purpose of life: making money, shopping and being comfortable.

How many times must Witney shoppers face this chaos?

Traders and the *Gazette* say: Call a Halt.
Some locals spat at cat protesters.

Traders in Witney say they are fed up with the "anarchy" of the town being taken over by animal rights demonstrators and are now lobbying for a change in the law. The town's Chamber of Trade and Commerce is pressing for a combined crackdown by the government, police and local authorities to stop a repeat of last Saturday's demo. Chairman, Mr Jonathan Russell told the *Witney Gazette* this week: "Enough is enough. This is anarchy. The whole town is fed up to the back teeth with it". "We don't want to stop their legal right to demonstrate, but they have a moral and public responsibility to conduct themselves within the terms of an agreement. On Saturday they broke it."

"There was supposed to be an orderly march from 3pm. Coachloads of protesters, and others in cars, came straight into town at midday and from then on it was chaos. If these people had sympathy for their cause, they have now lost it with their methods." Around 200 protesters brought Saturday traffic to a halt after blockading the town's High Street for an hour. The spontaneous action was part of an afternoon of demonstrations against the breeding of cats at Hill Grove. The unplanned demonstration went ahead despite an earlier agreement between the police and members of Save the Hill Grove Cats campaign, to stage a peaceful march later that afternoon. The sit in was condemned by Thames Valley Police. Asst. Chief Con. Robert Davies, who was in control of the operation, said: "We were very disappointed that the protesters broke the agreement and seemed intent on causing the maximum disruption to Witney High Street. Despite repeated requests from police officers, the demonstrators failed to co-operate and leave the town centre, and arrests were made."

But Ms Heather James, a spokeswoman for Save the Hill Grove Cats, said the demonstration had been a success. She said: "It has been a brilliant demonstration, and I am glad some people went into the centre of Witney. We are very determined and will never give in… The police have been very heavy handed. Some locals were spitting at demonstrators and giving verbal abuse, but none of them were arrested."

Mr Goodfellow admitted there was animosity between some local people and the demonstrators, but he insisted the police have acted reasonably. He said: "There are a wide range of opinions in the town, but we have to be impartial."

Many Witney residents answered this editorial, and again, the contribution from those people supporting the anti-vivisectionists was intelligent, informed and impassioned. They all put forward serious arguments against doing away with democracy and banning protest.

Battleground

With reference to the Hill Grove farm situation. I sympathise with both sides of this problem. But Witney should not be a battleground between demonstrators and shopkeepers. Both sides are angry, justifiably so for different reasons. Much as I despise Christopher Brown and his "profession" he, according to the law, is carrying out a legitimate business. The fact that it is cruel, barbaric and immoral, in my opinion, and should be stopped is never going to affect this individual.

The Home Secretary is responsible for giving out licences for establishments such as Hill Grove and it is at Jack Straw's department that the protests should be aimed. The Witney shopkeepers would be doing all concerned a service by joining the protesters and complaining to Jack Straw to remove the licences of Hill Grove and other places like it.

I think the *Witney Gazette* is taking the easy road out of this situation, brush the nuisance out of the way instead of attacking the root cause. If you ban the protesters, the cruelty to animals will still be there. I have written to the Home Secretary and received pompous replies. Given the large number of people who clearly feel strongly about animal cruelty there is clearly a good case for taking the pressure off Witney and pushing it over to the government.

There is likely to be strong national support for it and a far better chance of getting the law changed. It can be done! I do not object to the protesters. I object to Christopher Brown and I object to my community tax being used to enable him to carry on his disgusting business. I object to him purporting to be a Christian. I would like to think my local newspaper felt the same.

Mrs Shirley Coates - Lechlade[6]

Right to Protest

The Criminal Justice Act and many other pieces of legislation that have appeared over the last 20 years or so have severely restricted the right to freedom of speech and peaceful protest in this country. Now it would seem that some people would ideally like to ban protest altogether.

Protest is fundamental to the life of a free democracy. It is always the first thing that is curtailed and banned in countries with repressive regimes and dictatorships, so it is worrying to see the *Witney Gazette* advocating a "change in the law" and a "crackdown" on protesters. Votes for women in this country were won through protests such as these and I wonder how many readers would have supported banning the Suffragette Movement because their protests caused inconvenience to Saturday afternoon shoppers.

Martin Lawson-Smith - Witney[7]

---

6 *The Witney Gazette* August 11, 1999.
7 Ibid.

Who Are They?

Readers might like to bear in mind the contrast between the protesters outside Hill Grove farm, described by Richard Goodfellow of Thames Valley Police as well behaved and pleasant, and the louts of Witney, spitting and yelling obscenities at demonstrators. Who are the troublemakers? And why did none of the many police officers present make any effort to stop this behaviour? Impartial?

Trish Bowman, Witney[8]

Posters of Christopher Brown had been going up in the Oxford area. Many women working in pairs were busy all night; one did the driving and kept look out while younger, more energetic companions jumped out and slapped up posters. It is believed that the Browns received many phone calls as a result of this exceptional advertising service.

8 *The Witney Gazette* August 11, 1999.

Chapter Twenty Four

Total Victory

The cats are beautiful and a joy to work with. It will be a terrific wrench. I'm opposed to animal cruelty in any way whether it's for research or not.[1]

There were rumours that the RSPCA had been approached to rehouse 800 cats. Unknown to the campaigners, Hill Grove farm had been busy for some weeks. Brown had been trying, without success, to sell his stock and even the whole farm as a job lot. Who would want it – buy the farm and get the demos free!

Starting at 10pm on the night of the 12th of August, 1999, a carefully planned rescue was carried out like a military operation by the RSPCA. At twenty minutes to nine on the morning of August 13th Cynthia's phone rang, it was a call from a *Witney Gazette* reporter that she would never forget. "Cynthia, David here. I've just had a message: Hill Grove is closed. What do you know?" Then at twenty minutes to ten, the phone rang again.

"Suzanne here, yes, it's definite, he's closed."

Cynthia's phone was jammed with incoming calls for almost three days. The news spread rapidly. Sleep did not come easily that night; Cynthia was on a high.

---

1 Christopher Brown, *The Independent*.

The Happening

We decided to attend the planned all-night demonstration on the 14th August although we were already aware, obviously, of the brilliant news. Meeting by Burford Road car park at 9.45 p.m. we walked down Dry Lane together. As we walked carrying a portable CD player I played *Amazing Grace* by the Gordon Highlanders.

Being a dry windless evening, the sound of bagpipes echoed over the Windrush Valley. On getting level with Christine I noticed that she had tears in her eyes and that she was showing the same emotions as I felt. It was almost as if this music was like the "last post" in memory of all the cats from here that had been butchered.

On getting within 20 yards of the entrance of Hill Grove, none other than officers Petit and Lay drew level with me in a Range Rover and stared at me, trying to intimidate me into stopping the music.

We were surprised to find that there were already about 20 people outside the farm. Later during the night the number would increase to 40 or 50 at any time. Everyone was clearly up for partying and in a great mood; everyone, that is, apart from the police. As soon as they saw our numbers were growing, reinforcements were called. For no apparent reason they suddenly marched out in front of us and lined up in a show of strength. I played Bob Dylan's song *The times they are a'changing...* a real inspiring to any form of protest; I played it as loud as I could.

The rest of the evening was what was referred to in the sixties as "a happening"; something that could never be planned as it was so spontaneous and special. Champagne, wine and beer was passed around with food. Nothing could spoil this party, everyone was so happy. I will never forget that night. Of course we thought of absent friends who so deserved to see this night. Some were in prison and many on police bail, banned from putting a foot on the soil around Hill Grove. A long hard battle had been won!

Roger Lee

Victoria Plum and Cynthia had tried in a variety of unsuccessful ways to trace the Curbridge Eleven, arrested after the first raid on the farm. Around two o'clock on August 13, Cynthia received a call from Ann, who knew two of the original Curbridge Eleven. Twenty minutes after Ann's call, Maggie Morrison was on the phone. "I was one of the early activists. Many congratulations to you." Spellbound Cynthia replied: "We would never have known about this place were it not for you way back in 1981." With that phone call, the idea of an annual reunion was born.

Towards the end of the campaign Cynthia was receiving the deserved respect that the British State reserves for those of whom it becomes frightened. Cynthia was "an ordinary person" stirred to serious opposition to one small aspect of the medical-industrial complex. Everywhere that Cynthia turned in order to right the terrible wrong of vivisection, she found more injustice, and as the establishment closed ranks on her and employed the police, in the guise of protecting Brown's rights and freedoms, her anger became increasingly focused . She learned by experience all the lessons of political organisation which are not found in books. Not only did she have right on her side, but as Che Guevara once wrote, all revolutionaries are motivated by love and Cynthia's case was the stronger for this. Her example sent sparks far and wide and lit fires in the minds of thousands of people who would never normally have thought of demonstrating.

Perhaps even more importantly, Cynthia never let down the more radical elements which the campaign attracted; she never betrayed or disavowed them. Consequently, like all good campaigns, the Hill Grove campaign developed two wings and while one wing educated and agitated, the other kept the flame alight with a serious of actions which worried, annoyed and damaged the property of the opposition.

Once the tears and the emotions ebbed, Cynthia's view of the campaign which she had begun and been an example to for over eight years was summed up with a modesty and sincerity which had become her hallmark.

> Victory was bound to come. All social evils have eventually been overcome by protests and campaigns. Were it not for such campaigns, children would still be working slave hours in factories and used as chimney sweeps. It was my privilege to have been a small cog in a large wheel. Indeed it has been an honourable duty accompanied by sadness, tears, lock ups, fines and police harassment. I am very grateful for the laughter, the love, the real friendships which gave us the strength to overcome many obstacles and let us triumph. My mind goes back to the freezing cold early morning stints; my brutal lock up in police cells and of course that lovely spring day of our biggest demo of the time on the 4th of May 1997. Only twelve of us then but I remember the brilliant sunshine lighting up the faces of new friends.

> Still under court injunction and not allowed to stop my car, all I could do at the last, was throw a large bunch of flowers tied with a purple ribbon and a message from my car window. The ground was bare and brown where the protesters wore the earth away. I wondered if the family of robins would still come to Dry Lane expecting the sultanas protesters used to throw for them?

Cynthia's joy at the victory was slightly clouded on hearing that the RSPCA had, as usual, hijacked the event; why couldn't the RSPCA have saved the cats twenty years previously? The nationwide publicity given to this historic triumph would no doubt ensure that the RSPCA found the cats good homes, in contrast to their usual policy of putting down healthy animals or dumping them on the hard pressed and under-resourced sanctuaries run by dedicated individuals.

Maggie and Peter Morrison agreed that the contemporary activists should meet up with those of almost two decades before. A celebration lunch for eighteen was organised. The guests of honour had to be Peter and Maggie and a bouquet of flowers was presented to Maggie in honour of the movement's history. The two one-time activists now run an award winning animal rescue shelter.

It was a most enjoyable meal and the Manager of the hotel seemed surprised to see an ordinary, well behaved group all neatly dressed in party attire. The clothes were certainly a change from thick boots and heavy, warm, clothing of the protest days. A date was made to meet in the year 2000 and in the coming years when it is hoped even more people would attend. After some discussion the group decided to call themselves the "Early Birds". To qualify for membership of this exclusive club one had to have been a protester of the early days before "Save the Hill Grove Cats" was formed.

Out of the restaurant in Oxford City centre Cynthia and friends were conscious of Thames Valley police observing them. Someone suggested that they might make a last drive past Prof. Blakemore's house but when they reached it, their car was surrounded by Thames Valley police officers who proceeded to breathalyse them! Despite the fact that Cynthia never drinks alcohol, her reunion had an unpleasant finale when she was locked up, yet again, in Oxford police cells accused of harassment! Sound like sour grapes?

At Birmingham Crown Court on November 26 1999, three months after the cats had been released, Rose was again sent to prison with five other defendants. The charges against them grew from incidents in the Battle of Hill Grove. Dirty tricks behind the scenes ensured that all the defendants pleaded guilty. The parents of one defendant, who wanted to plead not guilty, received anonymous calls telling them to tell their son to plead guilty "or else!" A not guilty plea by any of the defendants would have meant that the undercover cops who acted as agents provocateur would have had to give evidence again.

After long discussions with their barristers about possible outcomes of the trial, all the defendants went to court in Birmingham on the 26th November 1999 expecting fines and/or community service orders. Instead, they were given heavy prison sentences. Which just goes to show, Cynthia said: "You can never trust the law to be honest."

Since March 1997, Thames Valley Police had spent £2.8 million protecting the Hill Grove farm and policing the demonstrations, around 350 people had been arrested and 32 imprisoned for public order offences.

Some of the luckiest campaigners were those who claimed kittens from the RSPCA, all the cats were gone in a matter of hours after the news spread.

> As a member of various English Symphony Orchestras, I've sat on concert platforms all over the world, but nothing will ever beat that magic moment when I carried Tilbey, our little crippled tabby into the garden for the very first time. Her little body trembling with wonder at the trees and the sky and the way she buried her little cheek in the grass and inhaled deeply the smell of soft damp earth. It was like a great song! Wonderful! It was a moment I shall keep forever.

That night after the cats were taken out, a beautiful red sky gave way to an equally beautiful sunset over Hill Grove and there was peace before the dark clouds of night rolled over the landscape. But listen! You can still hear the cats' cries. It is a haunted spot. Hear too the brave activists calling, the helicopters roaring overhead, the police dogs barking and police horses whinnying, the agitated police commands and a distant megaphone: "Vivisection will be abolished. Vivisection is scientific and medical fraud. We will win."

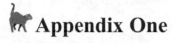 **Appendix One**

Facts to consider about the relevance of animal experiments to medicine.[1]

[1] Points 1 to 10 come from *Vivisection Information Network*, compiled by Cris Iles, the rest from *Quotations and Data for Antivivisectionists*, compiled by Jill Russell.

SEVENTEEN FACTS

1. According to the former Scientific Executive of Huntingdon Life Sciences, animal tests and human results agree 5-25% of the time. [*Animal Toxicity Studies: Their relevance to man.* Lumley/Warner (Eds)].

2. 95% of drugs passed by animal tests are immediately discarded as useless or dangerous to humans. [SmithKline Beecham Internal Report].

3. A number of chemical product companies, including Procter and Gamble have said in relation to a number of products, that results in animal tests are "of little relevance to humans." [*Ethical Consumer* Nov/Dec 1995, p24].

4. Rats are 37% effective in identifying what causes cancers in humans. Flipping a coin would be more accurate. F J Di Carlo: Drug Metabolism Reviews 15. [Quoted in *Vivisection Unveiled.* Dr. T Page].

5. The results from animal experiments can be altered by factors such as diet and bedding. Bedding has been identified as giving cancer rates of over 90% in the same strain of mice at different locations. [Pietro Croce, *Vivisection or Science*].

6. An estimated 83% of substances are metabolised by rats in a different way to humans. Drug Metabolism from Microbe to Man. [Quoted in *Vivisection Unveiled,* p. 45. Dr T Page]

7. Lemon juice and aspirin are poisonous to cats, penicillin is deadly to guinea pigs, but arsenic and hemlock, both poisonous to humans, are safe in several animal species. [Prof. Pietro Croce, *Vivisection or Science*].

8. Genetically modified animals are not models for human disease. The mdx mouse is supposed to represent muscular dystrophy, but the muscles regenerate without treatment. [*Access Denied.* Report, NAVS].

9. When the producers of Thalidomide faced court, they were acquitted after numerous experts agreed that animal tests could not be relied on for human medicine. [Hans Ruesch, *Slaughter of the Innocent*, pp.361-2].

10. The Director of the Research Defence Society (which serves to defend vivisection and animal experimentation), was asked if medical progress could have been achieved without animal use. His written reply was "I am sure it could be." [Personal communication, quoted in *Vivisection Unveiled*, p.101].

11. Imagine you've been taking a medicine regularly for around a decade, and then one day the government suddenly takes the drug off the market. For your own peace of mind you will certainly want to know the reasons why. Is it because new evidence shows it causes cancer, heart attacks, or psychiatric illness, for example? In Britain, under section 118 of the Medicines Act (1968), you will never know. Before deciding to withdraw or license a drug the government consults pharmacologists, toxicologists and other experts. Yet these advisers, who sit on the government's Committee on Safety of Medicines, could spend up to two years in prison if they tell you why the drug was withdrawn. They are also not allowed to tell you why they recommended approval of the drug in the first place. Data from toxicity tests on animals and clinical trials are considered too "commercially sensitive" to publish. [*New Scientist*, 1 October 94].

12. Our method is not confidential, and we need as much publicity as we can get, since there is a very strong commercial, political and scientific lobby to continue animal experimentation. This is very big business world-wide, and although most scientists who have examined our computer graphic approach to the safety evaluation of chemicals, agree that it is more scientific than current animal experimentation procedures, they are unable to use this because of outdated government regulatory requirements and certain vested interests of industry. [Personal Communication from Dr. D.V. Parke, Dept of Biochemistry, University of Surrey, 21 June 1990].

13. And after over 100 years of cancer research on animals, cancer has recently overtaken heart disease as the commonest cause of death in the UK. [BMJ, 13 Feb 1999].

14. And after over 100 years of medical research on animals, two-thirds of the 30,000 known diseases are still incurable. [Bayer advert, *Independent*, 14 November 1994].

15. By conservative estimates, animal tested – drug adverse reactions accounts for more than a tenth of hospital admissions. *Hospital Doctor*, 13 May 1993.

16. Despite animal testing (and we are often told that "this is to develop medicines for animals too"), many drugs, including the following sedatives, have not been licensed for animal use, eg Diazepam, Morphine and Midazolam or Torbugesic (for horses only). [*In Practice*, British Veterinary Association, July 1989].

17. Experiments in animals on Whiplash Injury are irrelevant to the syndrome, since monkeys cannot complain of the symptoms of whiplash. [J.W. Norris; Letter in *The Lancet*, Vol. 338: Nov. 9 1991].

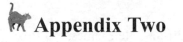 **Appendix Two**

Support groups and other information

ⓘ Information

■ **Animal Protectors' Bulletin**, Liz Long,13 Roseneath Road, London SW11 6AG England. Email: <114202.1657@compuserve.com>.

■ **Animal Rights Information Service**, James, P O Box 339, Wolverhampton, West Midlands, WV10 7BZ England. Email: <info@aris.org.uk>.

■ **ARC News -Animal Rights Coalition-**, Neil James, PO Box 339, Wolverhampton, West Midlands, WV10 7BZ England. Tel: 01902 711935. £7.00 for one year subscription.

■ **Arkangel Magazine**, Robert Cogswell, BM 9240, London WC1N 3XX England. Email: <arkangelweb@hotmail.com>.

■ **Awareness Publishing Ltd.**, PO Box 533, Sheffield, South Yorkshire, S11 9YU England. Distribute *The Cruel Deception* & *Science on Trial*. Photo-greeting cards for fundraisers.

■ **Campaign Against Cruelty -An Activists's Handbook-**, Alex Bourke/Ronny Worsey, Vegetarian Guides Ltd, PO Box 2284, London W1A 5UH England. Tel: 020 7580 8458 / Fax: 0870 121 4721. Email: <info@vegetarianguides.com>. All you need to know to run a group, use the media, run stalls & raise funds. £4.99 bookshops/online.

■ **Campaign for Advancement of Ruesch's Exposes (C.A.R.E.)**, 23 Dunster Gardens, NW6 7NG England. Tel: 020 7625 5935. Anti-vivisection campaign. Video: *Hidden Crimes*. Publ: *Slaughter of the Innocent, Naked Empress.*

■ **Civis –International Hans Ruesch Foundation Report–** nos 1-23. Civis, PO Box 152, Via Motta 51, CH-6900 Massagno-Lugano, Switzerland.

■ **Corporate Watch –GMO Website–**, 16b Cherwell Street, Oxford, OX4 1BG England. Tel: 01865 791391. GMOs in your area! A campaigning resource about test sites, storage, etc.

■ **Database on Vivisection Establishments (DOVE)**, PO Box 323, York, North Yorkshire, YO1 1RR England. Requests details of breeders, labs, suppliers, contractors etc. Local listings to be available.

■ **Let Down by Labour Campaign**, Mike Nunn, 24 Stafford Road, Seaford, Brighton, East Sussex, BN25 1UE England. Tel: 01323 490373 / Fax: 01273 490373. Email: <letdownbylabour@the-ultimate-answer.co.uk>. Parliamentary lobby campaign for local groups and individual activists. Detailed booklet available.

■ **SHAC (Stop Huntingdon Animal Cruelty) Newsletter**, 6 Boat Lane, Evesham, Worcestershire, WR11 4BP England. Tel: 0845 458 0630. Website: <www.shac.net>, Email: <info@shac.net>.

■ **SUPRESS (Students United Protesting Research on Sentient Subjects)**, P.O. Box 10400 Glendale, CA 91209-3400, USA. Tel: +1-818-790-6383. This organization distributes the most effective complement to Hans Ruesch's books: the 78 minute documentary Hidden Crimes, produced by Javier Burgos, founder and president of SUPRESS.

■ **The Civil Abolitionist**, editor: Bina Robinson, PO Box 26, Swain, New York 14884, USA. Tel: +607 545 6213. Website: <www.linkny.com/~civitas>. Email: <civitas@linkny.com>.

■ **Vaccination Awareness Network (VAN UK)**, c/o 347 Baker Street, Alvaston, Derby, DE24 8SJ England. Tel: 0870 444 0894 / Fax: 08707 418 415. Email: <enquiries@van.org.uk>. Information about vaccinations and their side effects. Support group, meetings, newsletter.

■ **Vegan Society**, Donald Watson House, 7 Battle Road, ST Leonards-on-Sea, East Sussex, TN37 7AA England. Tel: 0845 458 8244 / 01424 427393 / Fax: 01424 717064. Email: <info@vegansociety.com>. Educational charity that promotes vegan diet to benefit all: people, animals & environment. Publ: *The Vegan*.

■ **Vegetarian Society of the United Kingdom Ltd.**, Parkdale, Dunham Road, Altrincham, Cheshire, WA14 4QG England. Tel: 0161 925 2000 / Fax: 0161 926 9182. Email: <info@vegsoc.org>. Campaigns for children & adults. Local groups. Cookery school. Publications.

■ **Vivisection Information Network. Newsletters 1-8.** Cris Iles, PO Box 223, Camberley, Surrey, GU16 5ZU England. Website: <vivisection-absurd.org.uk>. Email: <vivisectionkills@hotmail.com>. Compiles and circulates the latest news & reports on medical & ethical opposition to vivisection.

📖 Books: difficult to get, out of print and available

■ Croce, Dr. Pietro –*Vivisection or Science.*

■ Hall, Rebecca –*Voiceless Victims.*

■ Ho, Dr. Mae-Wan –*Genetic Engineering; Dream or Nightmare. The Brave New World of Bad Science and Big Business.*

■ Lynn, Mathew –*The Billion Dollar Battle.*

■ MacDonald, Melody and the Animal Cruelty Investigation Group –*Caught in the Act; The Feldberg Investigation.*

■ Mason, Peter –*The Brown Dog Affair.*

■ Overell, B. (NZAVS) –*Animal Research Takes Lives; Humans and Animals Both Suffer.*

■ Page, Dr. T. –*Vivisection Unveiled.*

■ Rattigan, Patrick –*The Cancer Business.*

■ Ruesch, Hans –*Naked Empress: The great medical fraud.*

■ Ruesch, Hans –*Slaughter of the Innocent.*

■ Ruesch, Hans –*1,000 Doctors and more Against Vivisection.*

■ Ruesch, Hans –*Vivisection is Scientific Fraud.*

■ Sharpe, Dr. Robert –*The Cruel Deception.*

■ Thompson, Rev. James –*Cast Out of the Ark.*

■ Walker, Martin J. –*Dirty Medicine; Science, big business and the assault on natural health care.*

■ Wilson, A. N. –*Stray.*

■ **abebooks** is a good internet book search internet site where you might find some of the out-of-print books on this list.

■ The book *A guide to publications on the periphery* by Russ Kick -published by **Critical Vision**, Manchester, UK, 1998. ISBN 1-900486-03-2- is also a good alternative bibliographic source.

■ For all British animal groups, books, other publications and information, there is nothing better than the superb *Animal Contacts Directory*, published by **Veggies Catering Campaign**, 245 Gladstone Street, NOTTINGHAM, NG7 6HX, England. Email: <acd@veggies.org.uk>.

☞ Animal Liberation Campaign Groups

■ **Abolish Animal "Research"**, PO Box 24049, London NW4 2ZR England. Tel: 07759 114060.

■ **UKAVIS.** Distributors of *Vivisection Unveiled* and *Buddhism and Animals*, both by Dr. Tony Page. P.O. Box 4746, London SE11 4XF, England.

■ **Americans For Medical Advancement**, 8391 Beverly Boulevard, 153, Los Angeles, CA 90048, USA. Tel: +310 678 9076, Fax: +310 362 8678. Website: <www.curedisease.com>, Email: <AFMA@curedisease.com>.

■ **Animal Aid**, The Old Chapel, Bradford Street, Tonbridge, Kent, TN9 1AW England. Tel: 01732 364546, Fax: 01732 366533, Website: <www.animalaid.org.uk>, Email: <info@animalaid.org.uk>.

■ **Animal Cruelty Investigation Group**, Mike Huskisson, PO Box 8, Halesworth, Suffolk, IP19 0JL England. Email: <mike@acigawis.freeserve.co.uk>.

■ **Animal Liberation Front UK Supporters Group**, BM 1160, London WC1N 3XX England. Email: <info@alfsg.co.uk>.

■ **Animals Betrayed Coalition**, PO Box 21339, London WC1X 0NJ, England.

■ **Bantin and Kingman Campaign**, PO Box 29, HULL, East Yorkshire, HU12 8YA England. Tel: 07977 637293. Campaign against breeders of animals for vivisection, at Grimston, near Garton, E.Yorks.

■ **Brightlingsea Against Live Exports**, PO Box 1995, Brightlingsea, Essex, CO7 0EE England. Tel: 01206 304037. Reformed to educate the public, and to campaign against live exports (and other abuse).

■ **British Anti-Vivisection Association -BAVA-**, PO Box 73, Chesterfield, Derbyshire, S41 0YZ England. Tel: 01246 230474, Fax: Phone first, Email: <bava@esmail.net>.

■ **Campaign Against Fraudulent Animal Research**, PO Box 194, Enfield, Middlesex, EN1 3HD England. Public awareness campaign to highlight scientific & medical failure of vivisection. Supports BAVA.

■ **Campaign Against Leather and Fur (CALF)**, BM 8889, London WC1N 3XX England. Email: <calf@alrob.freeserve.co.uk>. Promotes the use of non-leather products. Campaigns against the use of wool, silk, fur.

■ **Close Kelbain Fur Farm**, PO Box 339, Wolverhampton, West Midlands, WV10 7BZ England.

■ **Compassion in World Farming (CIWF)**, Charles House, 5a Charles Street, Petersfield, Hampshire, GU32 3EH England. Tel: 01730 264208 / 01730 268863 / Fax: 01730 260791. Email: <compassion@ciwf.co.uk>. Campaigns for abolition of intensive farming & for non-violent agriculture. Publ: *Farm Animal Voice.*

■ **Covance Campaign**, c/o The Bear Cafe, 29 Rochdale Road, Todmorden, Lancashire, OL14 7LA England. Tel: 07960 992824 / 07949 349630.
Email: <siriussteve1@netscapeonline.co.uk>. Campaign against one of UK's largest contract vivisection labs, at Otley Road, Harrogate.

■ **Doctors and Lawyers for Responsible Medicine**, Joy Palmer, PO Box 302, London N8 9HD England. Tel: 020 8340 9813 / Fax: 020 8342 9878. Campaigns for a total, immediate and unconditional ban on vivisection on medical/scientific grounds.

■ **Fur Farm Campaign - Scabba Wood, Doncaster**, Mike, Tel: 0114 230 4435 / CAFT: 07939 264864. Campaign against mink farm at Scabba Wood Cottage, Cadeby Rd, Sprotbrough, Doncaster DN5, England.

■ **Hunt Saboteurs Association**, PO Box 5254, Northampton, NN1 3ZA England. Tel: 0845 450 0727 / Press: 07961 113084. Email: <info@huntsabs.org.uk>. Campaigns & direct action against all blood sports. Publishes *Howl.*

■ **Justice for Mike Hill**, PO Box 155, Manchester, Lancashire, M60 1FT England. Action against Cheshire Beagles hunt, after killing of Hunt Saboteur Mike Hill on 9th Feb 1991.

■ **Kent Action! Against Live Exports**, PO Box 363, Folkestone, Kent, CT20 3GJ England. Tel: Info: 01304 204688 / Fax: 01303 245228. Complete daily details of campaign against export of live animals from Western Docks, Dover.

■ **Mill Hill Anti-Vivisection Alliance**, Chrissie, PO Box 24049, London NW4 2ZR England. Tel: 07767 471111. Campaign against the medical fraud of vivisection at the National Institute of Medical Research.

■ **NZVS (New Zealand Anti-Vivisection Society)**, P.O. Box 9387, Christchurch, New Zealand. Website: <www.health.org.nz>.

■ **Protest against Harlan UK/SERA-LAB**, Loughborough Animal Concern. Tel: 0700 900 1853.

■ **Respect for Animals**, P O Box 6500, Nottingham, NG4 3GB England.

■ **Save the Newchurch Guinea Pigs**, PO Box 74, Evesham, Worcestershire, WR11 5WF England. Tel: 01902 564734 / 07814 488173. Website: <www.guineapigs.org.uk>, Email: <info@guineapigs.org.uk>. Campaigns to close breeders of guinea pigs for vivisection at Darley Oaks, Newchurch, Staffs.

■ **Save the Trafalgar Square Pigeons**, Tel: 020 8 802 2072. Help stop Ken Livingstone from exterminating the Trafalgar Square Pigeons.

■ **Seriously Ill Against Vivisection**, PO Box 116, High Wycombe, Buckinghamshire, HP14 3WX England. Tel: 0845 458 1720. Email: <info@siav.org>. Campaigning group of activists opposed to vivisection on medical & ethical grounds.

■ **Stop Huntingdon Animal Cruelty (SHAC)**, 6 Boat Lane, Evesham, Worcestershire, WR11 4BP England. Tel: 0845 458 0630. Website: <www.shac.net>, Email: <info@shac.net>. Campaign to close notorious vivisectors Huntingdon Life Sciences.

■ **Stop Quintiles' Animal Tests (SQAT)**, P.O. Box 127, Kidderminster, Worcs. DY10 3UZ England. Tel: 01562 745778.

■ **Students United Protesting Research on Sentient Subjects**, Patrick Rattigan, c/o Nemesis 1 Quarry Bank Road, Chesterfield, Derbyshire, S41 0HH England. Tel: 01246 230474 / Fax: Phone first. UK contact for USA producers of Hidden Crimes - the scientific fraud of animal based research.

■ **Uncaged Campaigns**, Angela, Lynn, Dan, 2nd Floor, St Matthew's House, 45 Carver Street, Sheffield, South Yorkshire, S1 4FT England. Tel: 0114 272 2220 / Fax: 0114 272 2225, Email: <info@uncaged.co.uk>. National campaign against vivisection. Several campaigns, marches, resource catalogue.

■ **Vegan Prisoners Support Group**, Jo-Ann, P O Box 194, Enfield, Middlesex, EN1 3HD England. Tel: 020 8292 8325 / Emergencies only / Fax: 020 8292 8325. Email: <hvpc@vpsg.freeserve.co.uk>. Moral support, practical assistance and advice to vegan animal rights prisoners of conscience.

■ **VIVA -Vegetarians International Voice for Animals-**, 12 Queen Square, Brighton BN1 3FD, England. Tel: 01273 777688, Fax: 01273 776755, Website: <www.viva.org.uk>, Email: <info@viva.org.uk>.

Index

SLINGSHOT PUBLICATIONS

Slingshot Publications was set up in 1993. The object of the company is to publish books, especially relating to campaigns, which otherwise would not get published. In 1993 Slingshot published **Dirty Medicine**; *Science, big business and the assault on natural health care*, and in 1998 the booklet **Loic Le Ribault's Resistance**; *The creation of a treatment for arthritis and the persecution of its author, France's foremost forensic scientist*, both by Martin Walker. In the coming year Slingshot will publish another two books by Martin Walker: **Skewed**; *Psychiatric hegemony and the manufacture of mental illness in Multiple Chemical Sensitivity, Gulf War Syndrome, Myalgic Encephalomyelitis and Chronic Fatigue Syndrome* and **The Gatekeepers**; *Attacks on alternative cancer therapies since the 19th century.* Slingshot is also preparing to publish **Slaughter of the Innocent** by Hans Ruesch.

Like everything else in postindustrial society, writing and publishing has been carved up by a few cynical multinational agencies. Slingshot does not want to compete with established publishers, or even become involved in the book publishing trade; we want to publish those books which have difficulty surviving or might not see the light of day, mainly books which have a relationship to campaigns or are written by activists. We are interested in handbooks, reference works on campaigning and books on particular subjects that grow out of community campaigns. We do not aim to sell our books through bookshops, but through campaigns, which we support, so raising money for these causes.

Books are expensive to print and distribute and consequently, Slingshot Publications is constantly underfunded. With
the last issue of *Dirty Medicine* and the first issue of *A Cat in
Hell's Chance*, the company tried to solve this problem by selling,
in advance of printing, copies of the books at half the cover price.
Dirty Medicine has, however, been out of print for about five
years now, despite continuing orders, because Slingshot lacks the
money to reprint it –its first printing cost £11,000 and the second
printing £15,000. Slingshot is interested in hearing from anyone
who is either willing to loan amounts of money for the first
printing of books or who will buy-up for further distribution large
quantities of books at half price or less. Anyone offering the
company inexpensive or free legal or accounting expertise would
be welcome.

Slingshot is interested in looking at well written and re-
searched manuscripts, which wouldn't normally find a publisher,
especially dealing with subjects in the field of medicine, campaigns for alternative medicine and vitamins, animal rights,
ecology, toxic industry and critiques of science or, alternatively,
life histories of those involved in these areas or other fringe
movements.

Slingshot Publications
BM Box 8314
London WC1N 3XX
England

Forthcoming books from Slingshot Publications:

SKEWED

Psychiatric Hegemony and the Manufacture of Mental
Illness in Multiple Chemical Sensitivity, Gulf War
Syndrome, Myalgic Encephalomyelitis and Chronic
Fatigue Syndrome.

Martin J Walker

Since the first clinical ecologists began to relate illness to
chemicals in the 1940's, and more definitely since Rachel Carson
wrote *Silent Spring*, chemical manufacturers have determinedly
denied that chemicals cause serious illnesses. In the early
nineteen nineties, however, it was suggested that exposure to very
low levels of some chemicals could cause chronic illness and a
life long vulnerability to a wide range of chemicals. To obscure
any connection between chemicals and illness, from the nineteen
seventies onwards, the chemical companies have argued that
those presenting with apparently chemically induced illness in
fact have mental problems. In the main, this view has been
propagated by psychiatrists. *Skewed* recounts the history of this
strategy of redefining mental illness to suit industry, especially in
relation to ME and CFS. It tries to make political sense of the
refusal by a number of leading doctors and psychiatrists to
research physical causes of a wide range of 'modern' illnesses.

Expected publication date: April 2003.

SLAUGHTER OF THE INNOCENT
Animals in Medical Research
Hans Ruesch

Slaughter of the Innocent is the seminal anti-vivisection book, the book which, together with its author's strength and campaigning energy, firmly established the modern abolitionist anti-vivisection movement. Various printings of the book have met with both critical acclaim and strategic censorship from the business and political interests which support the vivisection industry. The book has been re-printed on four occasions, the last time in 1991 when it was published in America.

Despite continual interference with its printing and distribution, the book has sold hundreds of thousands of copies and influenced a generation of animal rights campaigners, doctors and progressive scientists, throughout the world. In Italy, where the book was first published, the Stampa Sera newspaper said of *Slaughter of the Innocent*: 'A violent and well documented indictment against vivisection and its erroneous findings... resulting in a manufactory of diseases. An exceptional and courageous book.'

Slingshot is proud to be publishing the new edition of this classic work.

Expected publication date: April 2003.

THE GATE KEEPERS

A Century of Opposition to the Cancer Establishment in Britain

Martin J Walker

When scientific medicine came of age in the second half of the nineteenth century, it's professional organizations and its practitioners, scientists and physicians, turned upon traditional health therapists. Nowhere was this 'turf war' more aggressive than in the field of cancer treatment.

In the 1920's, when scientists found Radium had an effect on cancer, this battle between orthodox and traditional cancer therapists became more focused. At the start of the second world war, the British government passed the Cancer Act, draconian legislation, which forbade any non qualified cancer consultant from talking publically or writing about the treatment of cancer. *The Gate Keepers*, recounts the personal and career histories of a number of important alternative or traditional practitioners who have been attacked by the State, orthodox physicians and research scientists. The book, which inevitably includes a critical history of the British cancer research establishment, could loosely be described as a history of alternative cancer curers in Britain from 1850 to 1990.

Expected publication date: October 2003.

Orders for A Cat in Hell's Chance:

Less than 10 copies £10 per copy, plus post and packing (20% UK + 40% overseas). More than 10 copies £10 per copy with no packing or mailing costs. More than 50 copies £9.00 per copy with no packing or mailing costs inside Britain and reduced mailing costs to Europe (10%).

Quantity	
Total Cost in cheque	£

Name...

Address...

....

.... **Postcode** ....

All cheques in pounds sterling where possible, other currencies in cheques at present rates of exchange. Please make payable to **Slingshot Publications** and send to: **BM Box 8314 London WC1N 3XX, England.** Please send money with orders. No order will be returned without prior payment.

Orders for A Cat in Hell's Chance:

Less than 10 copies £10 per copy, plus post and packing (20% UK + 40% overseas). More than 10 copies £10 per copy with no packing or mailing costs. More than 50 copies £9.00 per copy with no packing or mailing costs inside Britain and reduced mailing costs to Europe (10%).

Quantity	
Total Cost in cheque	£

Name...

Address...

....

.... **Postcode** ....

All cheques in pounds sterling where possible, other currencies in cheques at present rates of exchange. Please make payable to **Slingshot Publications** and send to: **BM Box 8314 London WC1N 3XX, England.** Please send money with orders. No order will be returned without prior payment.

Orders for A Cat in Hell's Chance:

Less than 10 copies £10 per copy, plus post and packing (20% UK + 40% overseas). More than 10 copies £10 per copy with no packing or mailing costs. More than 50 copies £9.00 per copy with no packing or mailing costs inside Britain and reduced mailing costs to Europe (10%).

Quantity	
Total Cost in cheque	£

Name...

Address..

....

....**Postcode**....................................

All cheques in pounds sterling where possible, other currencies in cheques at present rates of exchange. Please make payable to **Slingshot Publications** and send to: **BM Box 8314 London WC1N 3XX, England.** Please send money with orders. No order will be returned without prior payment.

Orders for A Cat in Hell's Chance:

Less than 10 copies £10 per copy, plus post and packing (20% UK + 40% overseas). More than 10 copies £10 per copy with no packing or mailing costs. More than 50 copies £9.00 per copy with no packing or mailing costs inside Britain and reduced mailing costs to Europe (10%).

Quantity	
Total Cost in cheque	£

Name...

Address..

....

....**Postcode**....................................

All cheques in pounds sterling where possible, other currencies in cheques at present rates of exchange. Please make payable to **Slingshot Publications** and send to: **BM Box 8314 London WC1N 3XX, England.** Please send money with orders. No order will be returned without prior payment.